GOEBBELS

NAZI MASTER OF ILLUSION

"The book is fascinating and innovative...I read it eagerly in one breath."

— Yitzchak Herzog, President of Israel

"In-depth research—describing the power of the most fanatical, monstrous, and massive anti-semitic propaganda the world has ever known. A must read."

— Maya Gorodecky, Refusenik

"It provides a lot of answers—even to those who experienced the horror in the flesh."

— Abraham Vered, Survivor of Auschwitz

"Hopefully it will be read by those who do not yet understand the power of words."

— Reuven Miran, Author and Publisher

"The author describes the dark figure and the distorted personality of Joseph Goebbels, an agitator with oral rhetorical ability."

— Prof. Arie Naor

"I was extremely impressed and overwhelmed of the depth of research. It's written in a way that allures the reader."

— Eliyahu Yakir, Holocaust Survivor from Poland

"An amazing study of the most influential figure in Nazi Germany. A masterpiece worthy of praise."

—Yossi Ahimeir, Journalist and Publisher

GOEBBELS
NAZI MASTER OF ILLUSION

The Destructive Power of Joseph Goebbels's Propaganda and the Holocaust

Daniela Ozacky Stern

Lazar Institute for the Research of WWII and the Holocaust, Tel Aviv

For more information, address:
www.lazar-institute.org

First paperback edition in English 2022

Cover design by Rob Allen (n23art)
Book design by Allan Ytac

Cover photos by *United States Holocaust Memorial Museum* and *Yad Vashem Photos Archive*

Library of Congress Control Number: 2022902362
ISBN 978-965-599-901-3 (paperback)
ISBN 978-965-599-902-0 (ebook)

www.danielaozacky.com

"But if we perish, the whole German people will perish with us, so gloriously that, even after one thousand years, the heroic downfall of the Germans will occupy pride of place in world history."

—Joseph Goebbels, March 1945

United States Holocaust Memorial Museum, Courtesy of William O. McWorkman

TABLE OF CONTENTS

PREFACE

Many Germans saw the Nazi movement in its formative stage as a South German movement, lacking sophistication and intellectual depth, a movement that held meetings in beer halls, a movement assembled from a rabble of frustrated men, including veterans who had not adjusted to civilian life after their return from the "Great War". They would sit around pub tables and discuss their problems and the disasters that had overtaken Germany. In gatherings held at the "Hofbräuhaus," one of the breweries in Munich, Adolf Hitler would deliver energetic, sweeping speeches. In February 1920, he introduced a new movement, National-Socialism, aimed at fighting against those responsible for Germany's defeat during the war. He referred obviously to Jews, Communists, Democrats, and those who had signed the Treaty of Versailles.

Supporters flocked to Hitler's side, including one of the figures who would later be at the center of the transformation of the nascent Nazi party into a general German movement that appealed to the masses. This was Joseph Goebbels, a young intellectual and a native Rhinelander, a scholar well-versed in philosophy, political theory, history, and literature. “Because what was Nazism until Goebbels influenced it?”,[1] asked British historian Trevor-Roper, as Goebbels “conquered” Berlin, becoming the *Gauleiter* (head of the party district) when he was only 29 years old, and granting Berlin its power as the capital of the National-Socialist Reich instead of Munich —the party’s birthplace. Goebbels was the man who planned and arranged the conventions and large parades that drew the German public to the party. He also created the “Führer Myth,” which granted Hitler a divine nature, a ruler assigned from on high, and he saw this as his greatest propaganda achievement.

A central question in the historiography of World War II and Holocaust research that has gone unanswered is how the leaders of the Nazi regime managed to sweep so many people up with them?

Furthermore, after defeats and disasters, bombings, and sacrifices, how were those same followers dragged into oblivion with their leaders, especially during the last year of the war?

That issue stands at the heart of this book. The foundational assumption is that one of these Nazi leaders, Minister of Public Enlightenment and Propaganda Dr. Goebbels, caused this. He managed to pull the German masses together to support goals he presented before them, and when they stood at a dramatic turning point during the war, they continued to blindly follow him to their ruin.

Goebbels was a complicated man with a multifaceted personality. He kept diaries for over twenty years, from 1923 to his final days in the bunker in bombed-out Berlin, in April 1945.[2] He began writing diaries when he was young and anonymous, but his hobby became a true obsession when he served under Hitler's command.[3] He dedicated about an hour every day to writing in them. For years he would write his diaries himself, but a short time before Operation Barbarossa—the German invasion of the

Soviet Union on June 22, 1941—and throughout the years of the war, he began dictating them. Thus, every morning upon his arrival at his office, before the staff meetings of the Ministry of Propaganda, which he led, Goebbels would memorialize his impressions.

Every day of the war he would document in his diary the events of the previous day, under the headline: "Gestern: Militärische Lage" ("The Previous Day: Military Status"). Goebbels believed that "my diaries may be all that is left of my life's work. It will be my legacy to my children." He believed these documents would one day be a rich source of information to describe the history of the Nazi movement. He likewise planned to retire from politics at the end of the war and dedicate himself to historical research—to be the Chief Historian of the Third Reich.

After the conquest of Germany and the death of Goebbels, his diaries were taken to the Soviet Union, and only in the spring of 1992, with the fall of the "Iron Curtain" and the opening of the Soviet archives, were they made available to historians. The historian

Elka Fröhlich deciphered and edited the diaries, with funding from the *Institut für Zeitgeschichte* in Munich and the Federal Archive in Koblenz.

The importance of Goebbels's diaries lies in their providing World War II historians with a complete and extensive personal record, written as the events were taking place, by a man who belonged to the elite of the Nazi party and was close to Hitler. Other individuals in the Nazi elite wrote as well. Some wrote memoirs, others wrote fragmented impressions. Among them were Heinrich Himmler, Alfred Rosenberg, Hermann Göring, and Albert Speer, the Nazi Minister of Armaments, who wrote his famous memoir *Inside the Third Reich*.[4] The unique nature of Goebbels's diaries is their continuity and the light they shine on the internal events and the relationships around Hitler throughout all the years of the war.

Diary writing was a literary genre Goebbels was particularly fond of, and he even used it in the first novel he published, in 1929—*Michael*, and in publishing the book *From the Kaiserhof to the Reich*

Chancellery, which describes the sixteen months preceding the Nazi ascent to power.[5] The latter book is finish with an expression of hope for Germany's good fortune under Hitler's leadership:

> We sit together until dawn.
> The long night has come to its end.
> The sun shines again over Germany![6]

From 1934, the year this book was published, onward Goebbels ceased referring to Hitler by name or his nickname at the time, "Chef," in his personal diaries, and made sure to use the title "Der Führer." This epithet—"the Führer"—was set as the formal manner of addressing Hitler at the end of 1931. Goebbels insisted that the party members only refer to their leader using that title, to which he added a pseudo-religious meaning. He was also responsible for the popular greeting "Heil Hitler," which German public workers were obligated to use. "Germany is Hitler and Hitler is Germany" was an additional propaganda slogan from Goebbels's stable.[7]

Joseph Goebbels was a brilliant propagandist who decisively contributed to the success of Nazism. He understood that entertainment was the best propaganda and that it had to be provided to the German people specifically in moments of crisis. Even terrifying propaganda, of incitement and cruel attacks on those he defined as enemies of Germany, was no less than a weapons in the critical moments of the war. In 1926, after having been present at a performance about the Prussian general August Neidhardt von Gneisenau, by German playwright Wolfgang Goetz,[8] he declared he would never forget a line from the play: "God gives you goals, and you must not be concerned as to what they serve." Goebbels's goals in leading the Third Reich were clear, and he knew exactly how to achieve them to their fullest.

From the moment he joined the Nazi party until his death, Joseph Goebbels tied his fate to Hitler's, and was in fact a full partner in leading Germany during the war. He knew that Hitler's success was intrinsically woven into his own. Goebbels's decisive role in leading the Third Reich is especially apparent during the last year of the war, when Nazi Germany was facing defeat. Then, more than ever, his propagandist talent was shown as a force that motivated the Nazi regime and army, trying to attain the coveted victory, even when the situation seemed hopeless. Because of events at the front and the defeats the Germans suffered, the Nazi's spent the last year of the war accelerating the extermination of the Jews, in what seemed like a race against time. Here too, Goebbels and his Ministry of Propaganda played a decisive role.

This book will focus on the last year of World War II, which was also the last year of Goebbels's life. The period discussed stretches from May 1944, when nearly half a million Hungarian Jews were sent to be exterminated in Auschwitz, to May 1, 1945, the day Magda and Joseph Goebbels committed suicide, taking with them their six children, the day after their admired leader, Adolf Hitler, committed suicide in his bunker in Berlin. One of the notes in Goebbels's diary, written while in the bunker with Hitler as the Berlin he loved so much was being bombed into oblivion, is written with melancholy words that express despair and an acceptance of impending doom:

> The evenings pass now always full of work,
> but also full of worry...
> We must not hope that the nightly, nerve racking, air raids
> will end in the capital of the Reich.[9]

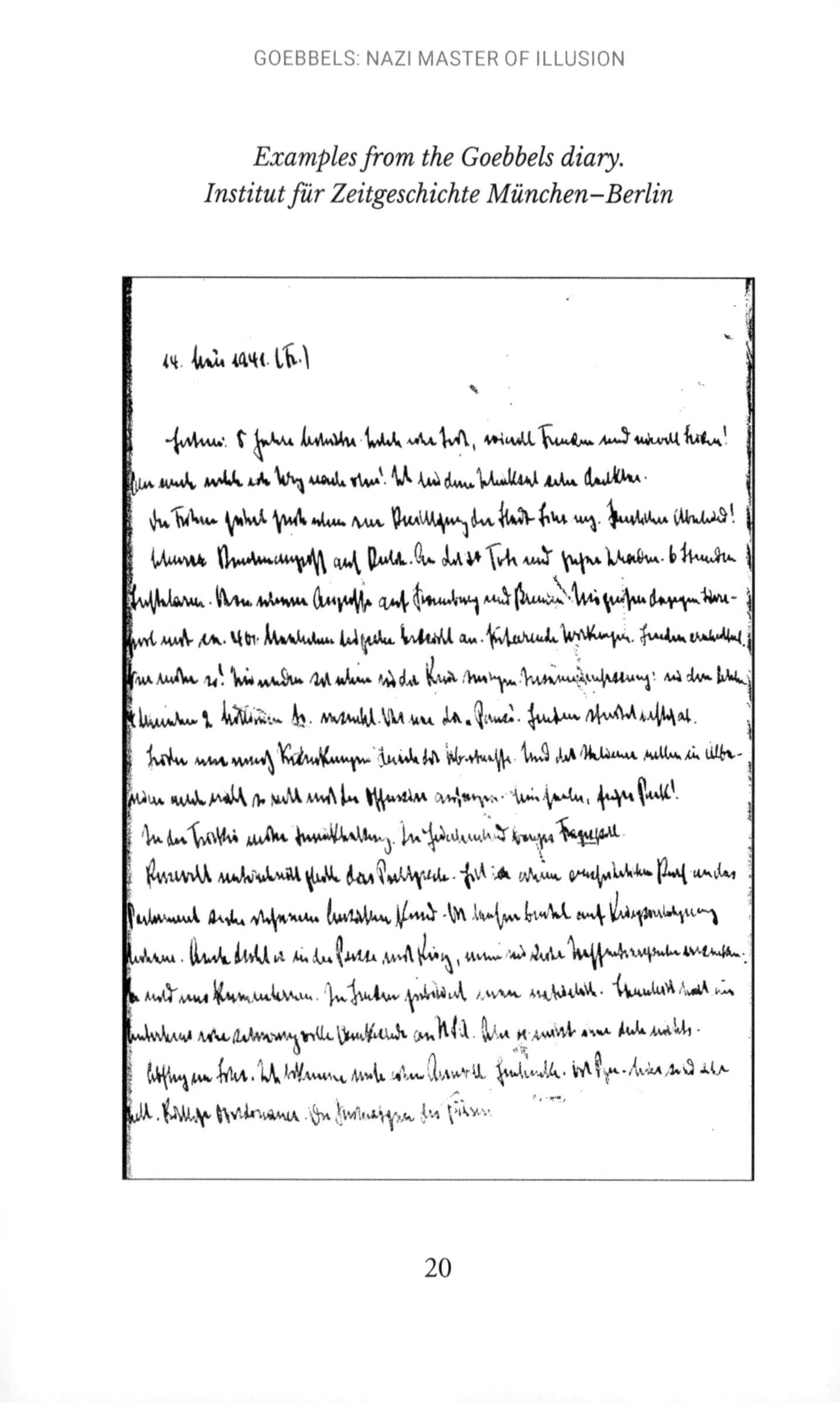

Examples from the Goebbels diary.
Institut für Zeitgeschichte München–Berlin

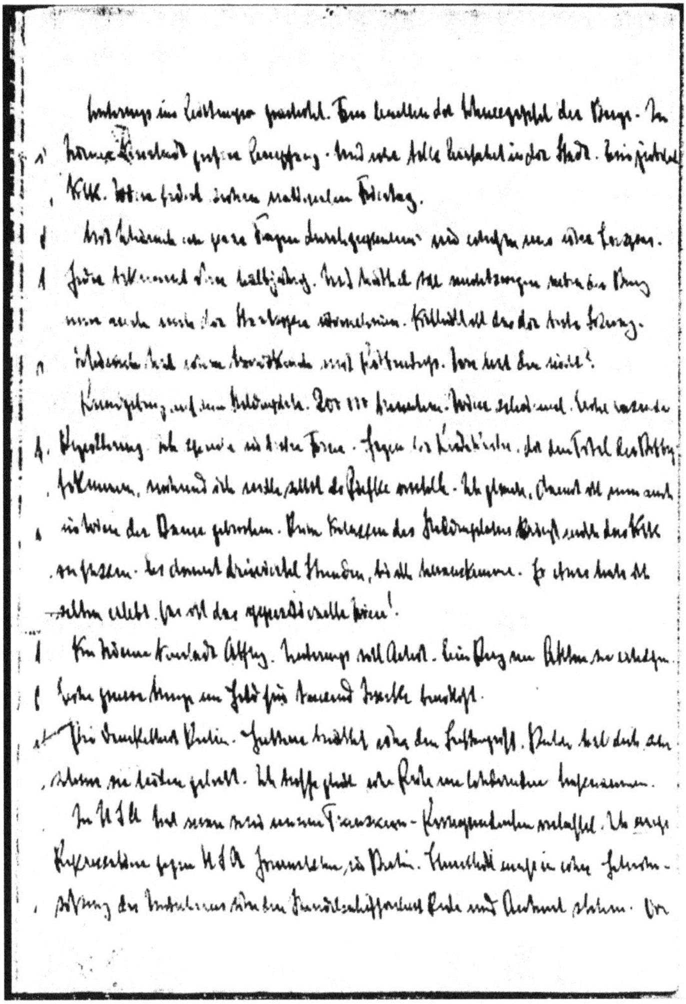

INTRODUCTION

The Legacy of Nihilistic Pessimism in Germany

In the prelude to his book *How do Wars End?* Bernd Wegner notes that the questions of why and how wars break out have been investigated much more thoroughly than the factors that bring about their ends.[10] While recent years have seen the publication of many important books that deal with the last years of World War II, it seems that little attention has been paid to a unique situation in the last year of the war. By this we mean the combination of the feeling of defeat and doom that the German Nazi regime experienced and the continued—and accelerating—annihilation of the Jews. This book will attempt to understand the connection between these two processes that might seem to contradict each other.

The Romantic movement and many of the European neo-mystic movements of the late nineteenth and early twentieth centuries rebelled against modernism and looked back to earlier times as utopian. Part of this involved what we might call "irrational echelons," hierarchies involving the individual and the state. With the rise of nationalism, the nation was presented as a kind of "supreme actuality" that took precedence over the individual. The nation was perceived as a historical, cultural, and biological unit in which the individual was only a part of the greater organism. Thus, the future and welfare of the nation became the supreme value. At the same time, a culture of pessimism and restlessness developed throughout Europe—and Germany—peaking after the defeat of World War I. The Great War reminded the cultural world that, despite progress and the Enlightenment and the conquest of distant colonies, there was still a deep affinity to barbarism within the heart of Europe. The sight of the wounded, the crippled, and the shell-shocked walking through the streets of the great European cities, after the World War contributed to an atmosphere of decline.

But in Germany, there were also those who produced a new and attractive worldview out of the "Great War," one that glorified battle and warfare, in which masculinity and brute strength reached their highest expressions and where blood and sacrifice had an added mystical value. According to this worldview, a heroic death in battle was more valuable than life itself. The death of heroes for the nation—*Heldentod* —ensured immortality for the warriors who died, in the "eternal hall of heroes"—Walhalla. Such a death was a valuable prize and represented the ultimate sacrifice for the people (*Volksgemeinschaft*).[11]

Many thinkers who were part of this trend of cultural pessimism also integrated anti-Semitic ideas into their perspectives, viewing Jews as the ones who would bring about the ruin of the Germans. They included in their writings nationalist, religious, and racial mottos. Wilhelm Marr (1819–1904), in his book *Der Sieg des Judenthums über das Germanenthum* (*The Triumph of Judaism over Germanism*), expressed a nihilistic pessimism that characterized the worldview of the radical anti-Semites at the end of the nineteenth century. His book, which became a bestseller in 1879[12] and was printed in twelve editions, was the first to express the claim that corruption and anti-social qualities were ingrained in the blood of Jews. Marr further argued that Judaism had turned German ideals into commercial goods and declared war upon them. The Jews had turned Germany into a land where they could look forward to a future and continuity, while the Germans had only the past and destruction. In this overtly pessimistic composition, Marr warned that Judaism was not just a threat to Germany, but to the entire world.

Bible scholar Paul de Lagarde (1827–1891) described the decline of German intellectual life in his book *Deutsche Schriften* (*German Writings*), which became an immediate bestseller with its publication in 1878. After his disappointment with the Christian religion of the time, de Lagarde called for the creation of a new German Christian faith, a national religion that would be the basis for a new state and a new society, where there was no place for Jews.[13] He seized upon the idea of the nation in a mystical way: the citizens would become a nation only if they accepted the calling or the divine task given to them, around which they would unite and become a people. He spoke of longing for a Germany that would be free of all societal evils, and he called for the appointment of a "Führer"—a leader—who would represent the entire nation and epitomize it. The Jews were, in his eyes, a symbol of degeneration, having polluted every culture in which they had lived, taken advantage of the human and material resources of their hosts, destroyed faith, and spread materialism and liberalism.

He further wrote that the Germans had only themselves to blame for being ruled by Jews, because they were too soft in their attitude towards Jews, and that they would have to adopt harsher policies. The penalty for continued passivity and inactivity towards the Jews would be the collective death of the German people. Thus, there could be no compromise with the Jews, and "they must be destroyed like insects."[14]

English philosopher and German sympathizer Houston Stewart Chamberlain (1855–1927) also presented human history as a struggle between the spirituality of the German people and Jewish materialism. The Jews and the Germans were, according to him, the only two pure races in the world. The Jewish race had always tried to gain absolute control over other peoples. Only if they were finally and totally defeated could a new world be created, and that was the "historic task" of Germany. Chamberlain published his book *Die Grundlagen des neunzehnten Jahrhunderts* (*The Foundations of the Nineteenth Century*) in Vienna in 1899, and the book was highly successful and received excellent reviews. It depicted Jews as a radical and evil force, and the author foretold that in the future an all-out war would be waged against them.

In this period of pessimism marked by a sense of degeneration, the anti-Semitic mindset cast the Jews as a plague and calamity for the Germans. It was no coincidence that the words of the German historian Heinrich von Treitschke (1834–1896), "the

Jews are our calamity" (*Die Juden sind unser Unglück*), were so widely quoted and frequently repeated.

It is possible that a similar sense of pessimism and nihilism hovered over the members of the Nazi leadership with their impending defeat in World War II. In the final stage of the war, of all times, the Germans persisted in zealously sending to the concentration camps whatever Jewish population had remained free until that point.

There is some dispute among historians as to the precise date when the decision regarding the "Final Solution" of the "Jewish problem" was made. The argument revolves around the question of whether the decision to exterminate the Jews had to do with the intoxication of German victories and conquests or was, in fact, a reaction to the first German military defeats.

It was about a month after Operation Barbarossa, the German invasion of the Soviet Union in late June 1941, while he was still confident of victory, that Hitler declared at a meeting held with party leaders on July 16 that he intended to make the conquered Russian territories into a paradise on Earth, through "any means necessary." According to the leading historian Christopher Browning, this utopian "paradise" meant creating a territory clean of Jews. It was the beginning of a broader plan for the "Final Solution." Browning claims that the decision regarding this solution was made between mid-July and mid-August 1941, while German soldiers were achieving swift victories, and Hitler gave orders to quickly purge the conquered eastern territories of Jews. During this period, the decision-making process that brought about the genocide of Soviet Jewry was completed, and Hitler himself gave the command to begin implementing the "Final Solution" for all the Jews of Europe.[15] According to Browning's account, Hitler did not wait for America to join the war before ordering the mass destruction of the Jews, and the decision regarding extermination as a solution to the "Jewish problem" was made in the context of the annihilative war against the Soviets: "Given the murderous atmosphere, the Jews of Russia had no chance of salvation from the fate meant for Communists, prisoners of war, and other 'undesirables.'"[16] According to Browning, the decision was made by Hitler alone, and he was the one who controlled the pace of development.

Christian Gerlach, on the other hand, believes Hitler chose genocide following the Japanese attack on Pearl Harbor on December 7, 1941, and the subsequent entry of the United States of America into the war.[17] Gerlach claims that the decision was made on December 12, at a meeting Hitler convened in his private residence. Senior leaders in the party and district heads participated, and the genocide was planned. During the meeting, he declared the decision to begin total annihilation, and so Goebbels wrote in his diary the following day:

> Regarding the Jewish question, the Führer is determined to clear the table. He warned the Jews that, if they were to cause another world war, it would lead to their own destruction. Those were not empty words. Now the world war has come. The destruction of the Jews must be its necessary consequence.

> We cannot be sentimental about it. It is not for us to feel sympathy for the Jews. We should have sympathy rather with our own German people. If the German people have to sacrifice 160,000 victims in yet another campaign in the East, then those responsible for this bloody conflict will have to pay for it with their lives."[18]

Tobias Jersak also presents Hitler as having personally made the decision to enact mass murder. When he despaired of a quick victory over the Soviet Union, he offered an alternative in the form of the "Final Solution." According to Jersak, the lightning victory over France was the turning point in Hitler's war plans.[19] Jersak refers to the section in Goebbels' diary from August 19, 1941:

> We talk about the Jewish problem. The Führer is convinced that his prophecy in the Reichstag, that if the Jewry succeeded in once again provoking a world war, it would

> end with the destruction of the Jews, has been confirmed. It is coming true in these weeks and months, with an apparently eerie certainty. In the East the Jews will have to pay the price; in Germany they have already paid in part and will pay more in the future. Their last refuge remains North America; and there they will have to pay sooner or later. The Jewry is a foreign body among advanced nations.[20]

According to Jersak, by "these weeks and months" Goebbels is referring to the signing of the North Atlantic Treaty. By this point, Hitler had already given up hope of a swift victory, and the "Final Solution" of the "Jewish problem," which had been planned for the end of the war, became a prerequisite for a German military victory. When the last Jew on European soil was exterminated, the power of international Jewry would be destroyed.[21]

In contrast, Ian Kershaw attributes an entirely passive role to Hitler in the practical policy decision making about Jews and claims that Hitler gave in to pressure and approved the proposals of others. Between September 14 and 19, 1941, Hitler authorized the plan to expel the Jews of Germany due to pressure from his Gauleiters (district heads), and during the months of September and October the mass murders began in the Soviet Union.[22]

According to Martin Broszat, no general order for extermination was ever given, but rather the process gradually developed and gained momentum on its own: Decisions were made to expel Jews in "other ways," specifically when the military situation in the East grew difficult during the summer of 1941 and the expulsion plans were delayed. Those other ways were acts of murder.[23]

Sebastian Haffner believes that, as long as Hitler believed he could reach an agreement with Britain, he limited the genocidal plans to the Soviet Union and Poland, focusing on achieving the principle of "Lebensraum" (living space). But in December 1941, after the defeat at Moscow, his illusions and his hope of victory over the Soviet Union were shattered, and he decided to achieve racial victory. He shifted to achieving the goal that was still achievable: destroying all the Jews in Europe. But for this he still needed to continue the war in order to buy the time necessary to accomplish this purpose.[24]

These different versions do not provide a conclusive answer to the question: Was there a connection between the frustration and vulnerability the German leadership felt due to their defeats in the battlefield and the increased motivation to annihilate the Jews? But they do inspire another question regarding developments in the last year of the war, when the German military defeat became a certainty. Germany suffered harsh blows in the rear lines as well, and nevertheless the extermination was accelerated. "In light of the severe shortage of manpower, it is difficult to understand the rationale behind the acceleration of the extermination process in the summer and autumn of 1944," Leni Yahil writes, "This clash of interests... reached the height of absurdity at that point."[25]

Indeed, the German military deterioration reached new lows during the Stalingrad campaign. During that campaign approximately 150,000 Germans were killed, 600,000 were injured, and 113,000 were taken prisoner, of whom only about five thousand returned home years after the war ended.[26] The battle reports from Stalingrad received in Germany spoke of the army's complete destruction after determinedly fighting to the last man. The blow Germany suffered at Stalingrad was a terrible low point, and represented a military turning point in the war. Depression and despondence were noted among German citizens. On February 3, 1943, the Ministry of Propaganda stated that:

> The German press stands before one of its most difficult tasks... the press must report this thrilling event that overshadows any other heroic act known in history in such a way that this supreme example of heroism, this ultimate self-sacrifice and dedication to a final German victory, will burn as a

> sacred torch. The German nation draws inspiration from the eternal heroism of the men at Stalingrad, demonstrating more nobly than ever the spiritual and material qualities that ensure the nation its victory."[27]

After the defeat at Stalingrad, the Nazi German propagandists led by Goebbels understood that the painful defeat could only be explained to the German people by reinterpreting reality through the use of myths. This was done in Goebbels' propaganda and was magnified towards the end of the war, when Germany's approaching defeat was granted a new meaning of ultimate self-sacrifice.

The losses on the western front, the loss of France and Belgium, and the growing difficulties in the eastern front, with the progress of Russian forces and the Polish rebellion (the Polish resistance movement was operating at full force during this period) were harsh blows to the Third Reich and marked the beginning of its end. The overall atmosphere was one of powerlessness, and faith in a German victory was completely undermined. Nevertheless, the army and the SS units went to great lengths to continue carrying out the combat instructions given to them by Berlin. Boys with no experience or military training were sent to fight on the front, and the German armament industry even increased production in the last months of 1944.[28] At the same time, instances of loss of control, disobeying of orders, and an atmosphere of lawlessness also occurred. For example, in 1944, SS men cruelly murdered French citizens in the French town of Oradour-sur-Glane and American POWs in Malmédy. On June 10, 1944, German soldiers entered the French town of Oradour-sur-Glane near Limoges, gathered more than 600 of its residents into barns, burned them alive, and then incinerated the town. Only one woman survived the inferno, and she told the story of the townspeople. And on December 17 that same year, German soldiers fired on a group of American POWs in the Belgian village of Malmédy. One can claim that these murders were not an expression of racial policy, but of offloading all burdens.[29]

In tandem with the military defeats, the German rear lines were also suffering difficult blows and tremendous losses due to Allied bombings. The state of aerial warfare (*Luftkrieg*) in the last phase of the war was dire, and the bombings even took on an "apocalyptic nature."[30] The mood among most of the German population was of despair and fatalism. Arguments against the Nazi party and its politicians multiplied. No one believed that the state of the war would change for the better. Those who spoke of hopes for a new weapon were laughed at, there were even rumors that "the Führer will use gas against Germany itself to destroy it." The civilian population also suffered from a lack of supplies and food, to the point of extreme hunger.[31]

After the attempted assassination of Hitler in Operation Valkyrie on July 20, 1944, the policies of the Nazi regime were changed, and with Goebbels's influence "Total War" (*Der Totale Krieg*) was implemented. This date also marks the point after which the face of the war changed: the "rationalists" in the Nazi regime, including Goebbels, understood they were not going to win the war, and now besides the external "Bolshevik" front, they must also face an internal front—German officers seeking to eliminate Hitler. Now it was valid to use all means to continue the war that was already lost.

One can see how, even as Germany deteriorated while approaching crushing defeat, its Minister of Propaganda Joseph Goebbels experienced an ascent and personal zenith, in which he used all his capabilities and skills. After hearing of the failed assassination attempt on Hitler, he helped organize a cruel slaughter of the conspirators. Moreover, he filmed their executions, so Hitler could enjoy watching them. Goebbels saw his involvement in processes taking place after the assassination attempt as a leap forward in his career. It strengthened his position, and he anticipated that, from then on, Hitler would accept his suggestion to change policies that were then current and adopt a more radical path Goebbels himself had unsuccessfully tried to implement immediately after the defeat at Stalingrad, at the beginning of 1943. Also significant are Goebbels's critical and condescending nature and his problematic and complex relationships with other members of Hitler's inner circle, such as Albert Speer, Hermann Göring, and the German Foreign Minister Joachim von Ribbentrop.

In the last year of the war, Goebbels's propaganda tried to provide rationalization for the continuation of the war, despite the lack of any hope of victory. We will examine his contribution to the line Germany took since the defeat of Stalingrad, particularly during the last year, when overall defeat was certain. Even when it was too late and victory had long since vanished from the horizon, Goebbels created the impression that Germany was still strong and could control its future. He justified continuing to exterminate the Jews, with one of his central claims being that continued fighting was to avoid falling prey to the "Bolshevik terror." Surrender would mean the enslavement of Germany to Russian forces with Jewish puppeteers behind them, seeking nothing less than the absolute destruction of the German people. Nazi propaganda presented the necessity of continuing the extermination of Jews and the war as a struggle "to be or to not to be" (*Sein oder Nichtsein*).

Thus, the question remains, was there a connection between the feeling of doom and destruction hovering over the regime of the Third Reich as it faced defeat and the acceleration of the Jewish extermination? In the summer of 1944, the last three large ghettos were liquidated: Šiauliai and Kovno in Lithuania and Łódź in Poland. In September 1944 the remaining Jews of Slovakia were also sent to Auschwitz. Half of the victims of the concentration camps died during the death marches and systematic starvation in the last stages of the war.[32] In this context we will examine Hitler's apocalyptic vision, in which he found meaning in the idea of self-sacrifice for a higher purpose. When Germany stood on the brink of doom, fighting the Jewish threat meant using any means necessary to eliminate it. We will explore the deep roots of the theme of doom (*Der Untergang*) in German tradition, and its connection to anti-Semitism.

We will likewise try to strengthen the central claim at the heart of these pages, that in the last year of the war there was a close connection between the impending defeat and the feeling of doom among Nazi leadership, and their motivation to accelerate the rate at which Jews were exterminated, all for the sake of completing the great task, the great mission of the "Final Solution." I claim that this was largely made possible by the propaganda mechanism created and developed by Joseph Goebbels, whose position among the Nazi elite and whose influence on the management of the war strengthened considerably during that last year.

Goebbels linked himself to events with a dramatic flair, and he continued his propaganda work in his private life as well. With the final downfall of Nazi Germany and the burning of Berlin, he performed a "Wagnerian" (inspired by the dramatic operas of Richard Wagner) finale to his life, committing suicide and taking his family with him on May 1, 1945, one day after the suicide of his Führer, to whom he remained loyal to his very last day.

CHAPTER ONE

The "Irreplaceable" Joseph Goebbels

Of all the Nazi leaders, Goebbels has perhaps the best chance of some posthumous rehabilitation and of a not-entirely vilified place in history's gallery of notable figures. He was the only one among them who did not deteriorate under pressure, the only one who in fact unexpectedly shone in crisis. From being a mere career man, an instigator, and a publicity man, he grew and flourished during those years when Germany was being bombed into defeat.[33]

Written by the German journalist Sebastian Haffner at the end of the war.

On July 25, 1944, five days after the failed attempt on his life at the Wolf's Lair, Hitler announced a new position in the German government: Reich Plenipotentiary for Total War.[34] He appointed Goebbels to the role. This was the height of personal and professional aspirations for the Reich's Minisetr of Public Enlightenment and Propaganda.[35] The night before, Goebbels finished composing a 50-page document in which he presented his plan to increase and radicalize the German war effort, a plan he developed since the defeat at Stalingrad in February 1943.[36] The new appointment gave him the needed authority to execute the plan, which until then was purely theoretical.

And thus, he got his way: Germany entered a new stage in its struggle—total war. "The German people have no other choice but to continue fighting fanatically," he declared after his appointment. The assassination attempt on Hitler was, according to him, the greatest test the Germans faced since the start of the war. It was even greater than the disaster at Stalingrad and the surrender of the Sixth Army under the command of Friedrich von Paulus on January 31, 1943, which marked the bleakest stage of Germany's military deterioration and the beginning of the end of the road towards Germany's total defeat. The German defeat in Stalingrad was a hard blow for the "unbeatable" Germany and a significant turning point in the war. After it, the Red Army held the strategic advantage. The principal cause for the German defeat in Stalingrad was that the German command was coaxed into a war of attrition. The German forces were stretched to the limits of their ability, in a topography in which the German military could not exploit its advantages.[37]

Joseph Goebbels. Yad Vashem Photos Archive

Goebbels stood out from the rest of Hitler's circle. He was exceptional due to his intelligence, his manners, and the charisma that radiated from him, in contrast to the mediocrity and crudeness of many members of the party and the regime. Alan Bullock claims that, among all the veterans who surrounded Hitler, Goebbels had only his mind and tongue to carve his path.[38] How can his complex character and contradictory behavior be explained? On the one hand he was a man of culture and an intellectual, while on the other he acted evilly and cruelly. Was he a cynical opportunist, bent on self-aggrandizement? Did he wholeheartedly believe the Nazi creed? Or was he willing to sell his propagandist talents to the highest bidder and to any cause?

Those close to him shed light on these questions from different directions: Goebbels was a man who "saw people as objects that can be used for political gains... [and had] a lack of respect for people," and who was only interested in control, as claimed during the Nuremberg trials by Otto Ohlendorf,[39] head of the *Sicherheitsdienst* (SD) Inland section in the Reich Security Main Office, and commander of Einsatzgruppe D. Paul Schmidt, who was Hitler's interpreter, described a different side of him: "On the outside he seemed intelligent, smart, and refined. He could have possibly been an author or a history professor." It has also been said that "his character has no historical equivalence"; that "he was the only one in the government who was irreplaceable"; and that he "always saw the bad side of every man."[40] Kurt Lüdecke wrote that "the radical, scrawny midget" seemed on the speech podium to be "a fantastical character, despite his grotesqueness."[41]

The harshest and most potent description of Goebbels came from his sworn enemy, Luftwaffe Commander Hermann Göring,[42] during his wait at the Nuremberg trials in 1946: "That limping fanatic! He forced women to sexually surrender to him by force of his political power. He influenced Hitler until he became even more anti-Semitic than he originally was... Goebbels was the most prominent representative of anti-Semitism... I think he was a liar, a thief, and too much of an opportunist to have deep feelings for or against anything... Goebbels was simply lacking a conscience, smart and dangerous... he was such a liar, there was no point in discussing anything with him."

"In Goebbels's case," wrote the historian Felix Möller, "all the qualities that had ever been attributed to him were probably true —a cynical, sly, brutal, intellectual, obsessive man, full of hate and exceedingly arrogant."[43]

In the introduction to his book, Curt Riess, a journalist and one of Goebbels's first biographers, claims that, when he asked to write about the Minister of Propaganda before the war's end, he believed it would be an easy task. After all, Goebbels had left behind speeches, articles, and many other manuscripts. However, when he began interviewing people who were close to the minister, he realized that these were misleading and claimed that "Goebbels told sweeping lies about himself, just as he did when speaking about the Nazi state."[44]

Paul Joseph Goebbels was born on October 29, 1897, in the small industrial town of Rheydt, in the Rhineland, which at the time had a population of around 30,000 people. His father, Friedrich (Fritz) Goebbels, a farmers' son, became the manager of a small textile factory. His mother, Maria Katharina, the daughter of a Dutch blacksmith named Michael Oldenhausen, was a simple, uneducated woman who could not even speak High German. Friedrich and Maria were married in 1892. They were devout Catholics and had six children, two of which died. Of the four who lived, three were sons —Hans, Konrad, and Paul Joseph, and one a daughter—Maria, the youngest. Another daughter, Elisabeth, died in 1915, at the age of 14. She was four years younger than Paul Joseph, and the trauma of her death haunted him for the rest of his life. Socioeconomically, the family was lower middle class, and they did not live in luxury. They had a duplex on Prinz Eugen Street. Years later, after the Nazis took over, the street was renamed after the local "hero": Paul Joseph Goebbels Street.

Goebbels was a handicapped, sensitive boy. His right leg was eight centimeters shorter than his left; a childhood disease left it paralyzed. This defect caused him to limp, which as a young man hurt his self-confidence. Due to his disability, he suffered humiliation and social rejection as a child, which led him to close himself in his room and avoid social life.[45] When World War I broke out in 1914 he tried to enlist in the military, but officials at the recruiting office took one look at him and decided he was unfit for combat. He enrolled in university in 1917, where, after seeing disabled students, former soldiers of the "Great War," he took to lying that he was injured at the battle of Verdun and that his disability was a result of that injury.[46]

The Goebbels family was a warm, supporting one. Paul Joseph was not oppressed by his parents, as many other children were in the patriarchal German society of the time. He was not beaten by his parents, nor abused, but rather spoiled and pampered. His high intelligence was apparent early in his childhood, and he was the only child in the family to receive higher education. His father had high hopes for his son, hoping he would become a teacher or a priest.

His mother was a religious woman. She adored her young, crippled son and devoted most of her attention to him. She took him to church every day and prayed that his leg would heal. He, for his part, agreed to go to church just to please her. She believed his brilliant intellect was a gift from God, to make up for his disability, and decided he should study theology. Her acquaintances were shocked that a passive woman like her found so much energy to realize her plans for Joseph. But her efforts bore fruit: her son won a scholarship from the prestigious Catholic association Albertus Magnus Society. He was even attracted somewhat to the idea of studying theology. But at the end of a conversation regarding his studies, the pastor turned to him and said, "Young man, you do not believe in God."[47]

It may be that, due to his loneliness and social rejection, he was filled with hate and contempt for the people around him, and sought to prove to the world and to himself that he was smarter and better than others. Knowledge was his superpower over those who mocked and disparaged him. He loved the idea that one day he would rise over them and control them. Even in his youth, Goebbels was arrogant and critical. He spent his time reading, sitting on his bed with his fingers in his ears to block the squeals of the children playing outside. Books became his whole world.

He was interested in German literature and romanticism. He studied philosophy, history, and art and literature history. He considered Fyodor Dostoevsky a mentor. He studied literature and philosophy in several universities in Germany. In 1920 he studied at the University of Heidelberg. Among his teachers was the converted Jewish professor, poet, and culture scholar, Freidrich Gundolf (1880–1921), who was part of the George-Kreis, a literary and academic group led by the poet Stefan George. Gundolf wouldn't agree to advise Goebbels on his Doctoral thesis, which dealt with the German romantic playwright, Wilhelm Von Schütz (1776–1847).[48] Ultimately, he was advised by a Jewish professor from Czernowitz, Max Freiherr von Waldberg.

Goebbels completed his thesis in only four months, in his home in Rheydt. The title of "Doctor" was very important to him from then on, and he demanded it be used in every public appearance he held. But in the first years following his studies, it stood in his way when he tried to find a decent job. His father could not even find a job for him in the textile factory. He moved back with his parents, and his father was ashamed of his son's failure. His friend, Richard Flisges, had a great influence over him at that time. Not much is known of Flisges, but the two were childhood friends.[49]

Goebbels discovered his gift for rhetoric at an early age. He would practice public speaking in his room, in front of an imaginary crowd. He not only suffered because of his physical disability, but also experienced failure when trying to fulfill his dream to be a journalist. His articles submitted to various newspapers were rejected time and again, but he never gave up. He admired Theodor Wolff, the Jewish editor of the newspaper *Berliner Tageblatt*, and sent him over fifty articles, but they were all returned to the sender unpublished. Ten years later, as a high ranking official of the German government, he had his revenge: He ordered that the newspaper be closed, and he forced the editor into exile.

In the first years after completing his studies, Goebbels was frustrated. He felt his life lacked meaning and had no purpose. He wrote in his diary that the revolution was inside him, but didn't know how to express it. He found his opportunity when he learned of the Nazi party and became a member in its early stages, in 1924. He was impressed by Hitler and realized he was about to perform something big. He wanted to be a part of that, a part of the creation of a new Reich and a new Man. He felt that he had found the purpose he was looking for. National Socialism was the new religion, he believed, and every religion needs a God. In 1929 he published his debut novel, *Michael Voorman*, which he had written in 1921. Many autobiographical details can be found in the book, including hints about his period of searching for meaning. Michael, the protagonist, is transformed from a confused romantic to a budding Nazi, from a sensitive youth to a grown man. Michael was both a poet and a simple miner. He represented the ultimate German man, a mix between Goebbels's friend Flisges and Goebbels himself. The novel has a chauvinistic tone, putting women in what the author deemed was their right place—in charge of the home and the kitchen. The answer the novel gives for the meaning of life is the idea of the German Fate (*Das Deutsche*

Schicksal). The German Fate requires total faith in the German strength, which is based on a glorious past and devotion of the individual's life for the good of the people. In *Michael Voorman* Goebbles writes:

> Therefore, it is Michael's life and death,
> That is more than coincidence and blind fate.
> It is a sign of the times and a symbol of the future.
> A life of service to the labor and death for the good of future people.
> This is the consolation,
> What we can see on earth.[50]

Goebbels's first contribution to the Nazi party came when France took the Ruhr region in January 1923. He took the opportunity to go to Elberfeld, the center of German resistance, where he spoke for the homeland. In his speeches he spoke of horrors committed by the French and agitated the crowd.[51]

David Welch writes that the Nazi party's reputation changed in 1927, when Goebbels employed his rhetorical skills in its favor. He and Hitler competed for prominence in that field.[52] When Goebbels gave his first speech in his hometown, Rheydt, he asked his father, who was not a Nazi supporter, to come and listen to him. His father answered that not even his son would drag him to a Nazi party meeting. However, Goebbels recalled how excited he was when, during the speech, his eyes found his father—standing behind the columns at the end of the hall, proudly listening to his speech. He was always sorry that his father died in 1929, without seeing his son rise to greatness.[53] His son Joseph wrote about his father in his diary: "Now I feel, for the first time, how much I loved Father!... He was a 'real man', quite the guy. Responsible. Zealous in his work...".[54]

Otto Strasser tells of his ability to give speeches: "For some time Gregor [Otto's brother] and I had been struck by the gifts of a young *Rheinländer*, Joseph Goebbels... with his unpleasant features and his club foot, Goebbels's appearance could certainly not be called prepossessing. But he was an extremely gifted speaker and had a flair for propaganda. We saw him at work and heard his passionate denunciations of the Nazi Party, and we realized that he would make an invaluable ally."[55] He added that "The unsuccessful journalist who had vainly peddled his articles round the German Press, the author who had been utterly unable to find a publisher, was now about to get his own back."[56]

Goebbels was indeed a gifted speaker. He spoke slowly, clearly, always looking at his audience, choosing his words, stressing important sentences, and using hand and body gestures and expressions. Before his speeches, he would take off his wristwatch and start speaking in a low and slow voice, so that the people around him would come closer and lend their ears.

Goebbels dressed meticulously and was careful to groom himself. He would do his hair every week, and would make sure his fingernails were manicured. Rumor had it that he had enough suits that he did not need to wear the same one twice in a year. He rode in a bulletproof Mercedes and would prefer to sit in the front, with his aides at the back.

Influenced by the long-standing tradition of German romanticism even before he was a politician, Goebbels wrote in *Michael* of the hope for the rise of an admired person, who will come out of the crowd to change the fate of Germany:

> I'm going to shatter the old world of faith
> Then, build a new world.
> I will start from the bottom and go piece
> by piece
> I wrestle with myself to find a different God.[57]

Goebbels met his wife, Magda, when she was the secretary of his subordinate, Dr. Hans Meinshausen. Magda was a beautiful, impressive woman, born to a wealthy and well-respected family. She had been married before to the industrial tycoon Günther Quandt. The two had a son, Harald, who was born on November 1, 1921. They divorced in 1929, but remained on friendly terms. Goebbels and Magda were married on December 12, 1931, in a Nazi wedding. Hitler was the best man, and the men attending the ceremony wore the party uniform. Magda's son also attended the wedding. Since Hitler was not married, after her marriage to Goebbels, Magda became the "First Lady of the Third Reich"—an example to Aryan women and the symbol of Germanic womanhood. The couple had six children, five daughters and a son, all given names beginning with the letter H, to honor Hitler, a frequent guest in their home: Helga, Hilda, Helmut, Holda, Hedda and Heide.

Magda was born in Berlin on November 11, 1901 and went to a Catholic school. Her father, Oscar Ritschel, was a construction engineer. Her mother remarried a Jewish hide factory owner named Richard Friedländer. Magda met her first husband, Günther Quandt, on a train. He was her senior, a thirty-eight-year-old widower with two children from a previous marriage. He courted her and she accepted, and even converted to Protestantism for him. Ello, Quandt's sister, became her best friend for the rest of her life.

Quandt was found to be jealous and demanded to know exactly what his wife was doing at any given moment. He was asocial and demanded she report all her financial expenses to him. After the birth of their son Harald, she took three more children of her husband's widower friend under her wing, after he threatened to send them off to an orphanage following their mother's death. And so, at the age of twenty she was a mother of six.

A rift between her and her husband grew until it was obvious that all they had in common were the children. Quandt's first-born son, Helmut, looked up to Magda and died in her arms after going through a difficult operation. To lift her spirits, Magda and her husband went to America, where she became involved in an affair with Ernest Hoover, the nephew of the President. When Quandt found out about her adultery, he threw her out of the house with no property or allowance, and she went back to her mother's house. Eventually, they signed a divorce agreement according to which she would receive an allowance for their joint son, with the condition was that the agreement would be null if she ever remarried, and the son would return to his father's custody. She swore that she would never again marry after gaining the freedom she so desperately needed.

A series of disasters befell her, and she had to revise that commitment. She was injured in a car accident, and after spending a few weeks at the hospital, she realized her life was empty and had no meaning. She was fascinated by a speaker at a Nazi party convention she'd gone to with some friends. He had first seemed like a small and sickly man, but when he opened his mouth and started talking, Magda was taken with him. She immediately joined the party and got a position as a secretary in its offices. Goebbels noticed her from the beginning. He asked around about her and called her in for a conversation in his office. She told him how impressed she was with his speech, and he realized she was a woman who could appreciate his genius. He stayed in touch with her, and they married despite her family's objections. Magda's mother never liked him.

Goebbels's marriage had its ups and downs. Even though a wife like Magda at his side made him seem serious and lucky, he used his position as Minister of Propaganda in charge of the cinema industry to have multiple affairs with young actresses. Goebbels had a lot of charm, and despite his deformed leg women were attracted to him. One of them was Czech actress Lida Baarova (1914–2000), who he met in 1936 at the studios of German production company UFA, when she especially caught his attention. About two years into the affair, during which Magda had given birth to their daughter Hedda, Goebbels brought Baarova over to meet his wife. During that meeting, he told Magda that he wanted Baarova to be his sole mistress and that they were in love. Magda threatened to complain to Hitler about it and asked for a divorce. Goebbels tried to discourage her from this, but she replied: "The Führer might control Germany, but not my marriage."

If things did not blow over at home, Goebbels planned to move to Japan and serve as the German ambassador there. After many fights, he left home for about a year, during which he only saw his children with his wife's consent.

Eventually it was Hitler himself who prevented the divorce: "You understand that a divorce is out of the question," he told Goebbels. "Do what you can to calm your wife down." He asked Goebbels to wait three months, and if he realized he could not live with Magda by then, Hitler would approve the divorce. The plan worked, and the Czech star had to go back to Prague alone. The relationship between the Goebbels couple grew stronger against the backdrop of the war, especially after the German side had suffered a few losses. Harald, Magda's son, was drafted to the front and given encouragement and support by the couple. Goebbels treated Harald as his own son. Harald was a tall, blond, blue-eyed soldier—everything Goebbels had dreamt of being.

However, Goebbels's most significant relationship was with his Führer. On April 28, 1928, Hitler appointed Goebbels as responsible for propaganda in the entire Reich. "National Socialist propaganda must be more determined, more fanatical and of a tougher meaning. In addition, it must also be updated," Goebbels said.

He also made a crucial contribution in this area and in attracting the masses to vote for the Nazi party at the stage of seizing the party's power (Machtergreifung), on January 30, 1933 and appointing Hitler as chancellor. In order to appear calm and assured of victory on the night of the elections, the Führer and Joseph and Magda Goebbels went to see the opera *The Valkyrie*,[58] from *The Ring of the Nibelungs*, by Richard Wagner.[59]

In a speech on the radio after the party came to power, Goebbels said: "On January 30, the national revolution began. This revolution will not stop at anything. It changed politics and carried out the reform of the German people from A to Z. Adolf Hitler is the man behind this movement. The period in which we live is of historical importance. We are steadily advancing towards a revolution in Germany whose dimensions cannot be calculated. The revolution has won! Its results will produce new political conditions in Germany. Now people have once again self-respect, work and bread."

Almost two and a half months later, on March 13, he was appointed to head the Reich Ministry of Public Enlightenment and Propaganda (*Reichsministerium für Volksaufklärung und Propaganda—RMVP*).

At the age of 35, Goebbels became the youngest man in the world to hold a position of such power. In 1935 he refurbished his office, at the cost of 85,000 marks. On one side of his office there was a large fireplace, and on the other a desk covered in red leather. To the left of the desk he hung a portrait of Frederick the Great. He would come to work carrying two briefcases: one with the ministry's documents, and the other with his personal ones. They were put side by side on his desk, at exactly the same distance from either end. His secretaries were told to sharpen his pencils before work, and his aides were instructed to prepare for him a summary of the news every day.

Goebbels's status and power reflect the merging of party and country in Nazi Germany; Goebbels was Berlin's gauleiter, Minister of Propaganda, and head of the party's propaganda office *(Reichspropagandaleitung,* or *RPL*), a body comprising departments for journalism, radio, cinema, and other media.[60] His appointment as the Berlin district's gauleiter opened up a whole new window of opportunities for him, which he knew how to take advantage of, thanks to his wit and ambition. The merging of the country and its Führer was created largely through his influence, since he was the one who formed and developed the "Führer Myth." Goebbels was responsible for Hitler's image as the leader Germany had been waiting for, the true leader, the liberator of the masses, embodying the mysterious longing for the German past, a guide to the belief that "before our eyes, [he] had performed the miracle of enlightenment and belief, as a meteor, in a world of doubts and despair."[61] As an author and creator influenced by the long-lasting Germanic Romantic tradition, long before he became a politician, Goebbels expressed in his book *Michael* a desire for an adored figure who would rise from the crowd and change the fate of Germany. I'm going to shatter the old world of faith Then, build a new world. I will start from the bottom and go piece by piece I wrestle with myself to find a different God.[62]

Then, after Hitler's rise to power, Goebbels explained to the masses: "You see before you a man who is the Führer of the nation and the country. He is simultaneously its strongest and most understanding defender." He compared Hitler's success and rise to power to the unification of Germany by Otto von Bismarck in the period 1870–1871. Hitler was "the symbol of the new socialist national unity." Hitler was the star of Goebbels's propaganda, more than a man, but not quite a god, the one Germany had been waiting for. Goebbels was the one who conceived the idea of the mystical connection between Hitler and Divine Providence; God had elevated him from the masses to lead the supreme race and was now guiding him on his historic mission. Without Hitler there would be no National Socialism. This was the dogma Goebbels had created.[63]

Goebbels's adoration of Hitler was more than a propaganda stunt or a ruse to advance his personal interests. According to historian and editor of

Goebbels's diaries, Elka Fröhlich, Hitler was a great prophet in the eyes of Goebbels.[64] Here is an example of what Goebbels wrote about Hitler in his diary from July 1944: "We have to love him. He is the greatest historical genius of his time. Together with him, we will march to victory or suffer a heroic doom."[65]

But, other than that adored genius, there were other members of the party Goebbels had to deal with. From the very beginning, the intellectual had a hard time fitting into that group. He was hostile towards Göring and his well-kept appearance, and even envied him; he called Rudolf Hess narrow-minded; he avoided Himmler and even feared him. He didn't like Robert Ley or Julius Streicher; he found Wilhelm Frick, the Reich's Minister of the Interior, too bureaucratic and pedantic.[66] Goebbels would constantly complain about the inefficiency of many of the party's personnel and would always recommend getting rid of one figure or another.

One of the people he constantly tried to remove was Göring, whom Goebbels persistently criticized and insulted behind his back. However, he also knew how to change his tune for momentary personal interest. For instance, after a friendly visit to Göring's estate, he wrote: "His house stands tall on the mountain, surrounded by wintry serenity. Göring himself was most warm to welcome me... he wore a baroque-style garment that, for those who do not know him, might cause them to chuckle... but they do have to accept his originality."[67] Goebbels would also defame and criticize other party members along with Göring, especially "The Three Holy Kings," as Göring referred to Hans Heinrich Lammers, Martin Bormann, and Wilhelm Keitel.[68] When he met Himmler, he had things to say about Göring: "At noon I went to Himmler for a long conversation. The ride through Berlin almost overwhelmed me. It had been a long time since I saw the destroyed fields that the Reich's capital had become... Himmler's approach is a good one. He belongs with the strongest of us... we agree about the financial situation... he used harsh language against Göring and Ribbentrop, who he says are origins of the mistake in our overall management of the war, which he is completely right about. But just like me, he does not know how to convince the Führer to get rid of them both."[69] Even when witnessing the demolished Berlin with his own eyes, he still found time to speak ill of his fellow party members.

For their part, they often voiced their negative opinions about him. This, for instance, is what Martin Bormann[70] wrote to his wife: "I have spent the afternoon with Speer for about three hours, in the evening he went to visit Reichsmarschall [Göring], with whom he meets quite often, and they share a joint antagonism. For instance, they both can't stand Goebbels."[71]

Goebbels was an intellectual; unlike other party members, he did not carry a gun, and he preferred the world of literature and culture to the battlefield. However, his language was cruel, and he knew the power of words, so he used harsh language against his adversaries, even when they were among those closest to him. He would often speak of Himmler's poor aesthetics: "It is obvious that Goebbels did not like Himmler... the well-mannered Goebbels could not tolerate 'unaesthetic people.' He placed Himmler in this category. "The Asian slant of his eyes, his short and chubby fingers, and his dirty nails outraged him," wrote Rudolf Semmler, who worked with Goebbels at the Ministry of Propaganda, in his memoirs.[72]

Goebbels complained about the temptations—spending and corruption—that were an inseparable part of the regime. Unlike his colleagues, he saw himself as honest: "A man should have a very strong personality in order to avoid temptation," he wrote with pride.[73]

Goebbels had his opportunity to show his loyalty to the regime and the nation on the afternoon of July 20, 1944. It was also a priceless opportunity to prove his importance to the regime and to press Hitler to grant him more authority. On that day, Colonel Claus Schenk Graf von Stauffenberg and other German officers attempted to assassinate Hitler by placing a bomb in his office, in what was called Operation Valkyrie. Hitler was saved by chance, but the event shook the top of the Nazi regime. Such a conspiracy, coming from "within," demanded policy change. Goebbels identified an opportunity to press

Hitler. He formed an alliance with Speer, and together they cooperated to convince Hitler that "Total War" must be enacted immediately, and that it would even gain public support.[74] "Crazy times call for crazy measures," Goebbels said.[75]

It's interesting to note that, when Goebbels could not locate Himmler that day, he believed that he was the one behind the attempted assassination.[76] Goebbels doubted Himmler's loyalty, while Hitler defended him until late April 1945, when he discovered to his horror that his "Loyal Heinrich," as he had call him, conducted negotiations with the Allies, offering unconditional surrender on Germany's part. Hitler called this no less than "a crime without parallel in German history."[77]

Goebbels's status rose on the backs of his opponents following the failed assassination attempt. His prestige was now at its peak.[78] This event pointed to the lack of faith the generals themselves had in the regime. This lack of faith was the root of the generals' inability to manage the war in the field. Goebbels was at his best when he gave the event the national significance that would lead to the unification of the people and its leaders in a fateful and mystical convergence. July 20 was a turning point in the war, and in Goebbels's status as well. This is what he wrote in his diary: "In fact, July 20 is not just the lowest point of an already crises-stricken war, but the determining day of our re-ascension."[79] He saw himself as an expert on managing crises, and even though the "generals' crisis" was a completely different sort that required special treatment, he was able to deal with it, among other things, by intensive propaganda. Semmler claimed that, at lunch that day, "Goebbels seemed pale and did not say a word. But we were accustomed to this behavior on his part."[80]

In his first mention of the attempted assassination, in an address to the nation on July 26, 1944, Goebbels tried to restore the public faith in the system and in Hitler's control: "I owe the German people a true report of the events of July 20 and the conclusion we must draw from them," he said. "The German people have reason to reassure themselves of the certainty of the upcoming victories of our righteous cause, which has the grace of God... I am convinced that no disaster and no danger would not eventually play to our benefit." He added that, when he heard what had happened: "For a moment I felt as if the ground started to open under my feet. I saw in my mind's eye apocalyptic visions of the historical possibility which could have befallen our nation, and moreover, the whole of Europe, if this cowardly and despicable act of terror had succeded. But then an almost religious, anxious, thought filled my heart. I thought it many times in the past—but never so clearly and undeniably as here—that the Führer will fulfill his mission under the protection of providence, and that no despicable or contemptible act could undermine or stop him."[81]

That day, Goebbels wrote in his diary of a report by the Security Police regarding the people's reaction to the conspiracy: "The report mentions absolute unity in all layers of the German Volk. Loyalty to the Führer is expressed as it never was before. There is the impression that there was a great victory here. Without a doubt the nation is now headed towards

Total War."[82] Goebbels became the most prominent advocate of radical policy and total war. He played the part of the *Psychologischer Diktator* (psychological dictator), who must work for the total effort by exerting pressure on public opinion.[83]

Goebbels's prestige was now at its peak, he was irreplaceable among the leadership, and his head was full of new ideas. Albert Speer and Goebbels were the two Nazi leaders who best understood Germany's situation at the time. They both saw it as an opportunity to take advantage of national weakness and act to advance their careers. Hitler's authorization to take radical actions was necessary in order for them to execute their plan. This was the way to guarantee the survival of the Nazi regime. And for that, Goebbels was willing to make promises to the German people he had no intention of keeping.

In October of 1944, Goebbels wrote in a newspaper article: "War has increasingly become a race against time... a national forceful effort which grips the entire German people and carries it away... the war is now at its dramatic breaking point. Without trembling or hesitating, our soldiers must fend off the enemy's advance at our borders, and the entire nation must stand behind them as if they were one person. The enemy must know what awaits them... it is our sacred homeland that we defend today... those who would die now will give their lives for the people... no victim will be too great or important for us. We have to hold this belief before our eyes like a banner."[84]

In order to start the "Total War," conditions had to be met in terms of the wartime economy and its efficient organization, and in assuring the people's readiness for war and strengthening their will and power to overcome hardship. This could be done through education and propaganda that stressed common foundations and strong leadership that would lead and spread the emotional and technical forces needed for such a war.

The term *total* has meanings beyond material ones—it is related to the self-awareness of the German Volk, who know their heritage and the potential embodied in it. If the German nation could create for itself a closed community, free of any foreign elements, it could reach the height of its development.[85] At that point in the war, military force was not the only important thing for Germany's struggle, so was the mental and national cohesion at home. The civilians must be in danger just as much as the soldiers.

In a regime meeting the Nazi ideal, the ultimate authority would be in the hands of the army's supreme commander (*Feldherr*), who would set policy. In Nazi Germany that "warlord" was, of course, Hitler, but Goebbels asked to take on some power and responsibility himself, so that he too could influence the war and its policy.

After the German Army's defeat in Stalingrad in February 1943, Goebbels suggested to Hitler that he radicalize the government's policy to implement a war economy, that he ensures the people's readiness for war through education and propaganda, and that he enact a firmer interior policy. He asked Hitler to be granted the responsibility for leading the war effort, but was refused. Subsequently, wiser by experience, he explained to his associates, that "if I had received these powers when I wanted them so badly, then victory would be in our pockets today, and the war would probably be over. But it takes a bomb under his arse to make Hitler see reason."[86]

As mentioned, there was a dispute between Goebbels and Hitler, which started right after the defeat at Stalingrad. At ministerial meetings in his office, Goebbels then stressed that only a more radical civilian war effort would bring about change in the military situation in the field.[87] After July 20, the regime's initial goal was to capture and punish traitors. The night Hitler was saved, an inquiry committee was assembled. It was headed by Goebbels, and officers and generals were investigated throughout the night about the assassination attempt.

Heinz Linge, the SS officer who was Hitler's personal servant, tells of the terror Goebbels employed after the event: "Men of every rank and distinction, who had put their lives on the line for Hitler, were suddenly treated like thieves caught in the act."[88] The historian Ian Kershaw claims that the 200 executions of conspirators were Hitler's last triumph.[89] I will argue here that it was also Goebbels first triumph in his new position as the Reich's Representative for Total War, a triumph which reinforced his political standing and brought him closer to Hitler. He took care to photograph and document the conspirator's trials and executions, so he could look at them later with Hitler. Historian Joachim Fest mentions that this nightly movie marathon created a feeling "as though sacrifices were being offered to some pagan demigod."[90]

"Had my life ended," Hitler referred to his miraculous saving, "for me... it would only mean being released from worry, from sleepless nights, and a harsh nerve disease. It only lasts a second, and then you are delivered from all that and find eternal peace and rest." He ordered that the generals must suffer punishment "of historical proportions." "The Führer was determined to eradicate the entire sect of generals who opposed him," wrote Goebbels in his diary, "in order to demolish the wall that had been artificially built by this gang of generals, with the army on one side and the party and the people on the other."[91]

However, despite those few rotten apples discovered around Hitler, the coming together of the party following the assassination attempt gave it new life, for a while. The Führer, who had escaped certain death, now reclaimed his divine glory, and Goebbels continued to admire and believe in him.[92] Hitler had once again felt his sense of calling, as he told Benito Mussolini, who came to visit him that day: "After having escaped the danger of death today, I am certain—more than before—that my calling is to continue our joint endeavor and bring it to a successful conclusion."[93] He had received yet another confirmation of his being the man meant to lead the Germans to their final triumph.[94]

But Germany's victory was nowhere in sight at that point, and now it was clear to Hitler why his military plans failed—the traitorous army officers sabotaged them the whole time. It was all treason! It was a wonderful excuse for Germany's difficult military situation, an excuse that left Hitler, as he said himself, free of responsibility for the deteriorating situation. On August 3, 1944, Goebbels wrote in his diary: "The generals don't oppose Hitler because of the crises we experience in the front; on the contrary, we experience crises at the front because of the generals' opposition to the Führer."[95]

One of Hitler's senior officers, Nicolaus von Below, wrote that 1944 ended with a feeling of hopelessness.[96] Goebbels, who was in charge of the popular moral, had to deal with that atmosphere. Since he could no longer rely on military victories, all he had left to mention was the recovery and rebirth of the German nation from the depth of catastrophe. He saw in the generals' attempted military *coup d'état* a low point from which Germany could only move up. He believed this crisis would strengthen the German people's resistance, rather than weaken it. But danger still existed: If the Führer were injured, it would have been only a matter of time before the Bolsheviks would have taken over Europe, he wrote in his diary.[97] In an article from early January, 1945, he wrote: "July 20 last year illustrated the deep German crisis. From there on, the production of the German military defensive and offensive force began, slowly but surely... God would help us if we would help ourselves. He stands not with the strongest battalions, but with the bravest."[98]

As mentioned, a strict policy was enacted on the German home front. Every citizen within working age, man or woman, was required to fight or work for the homeland. Ultimate victory is still in reach, Goebbels argued, through a combined effort on the war-front and the home-front. In his attempt to apply a "Total War" policy, Goebbels was faced with discord between ideological needs and technical ones. Economic rationality, represented by Speer, demanded focus on material resources and maximization of production. Goebbels, on the other hand, thought that the deterioration of the military situation was the result of ideological disloyalty on the part of the people, and this is what must be emphasized. The two had a harsh argument on the subject.[99] According to Goebbels, the importance was "not only on the technology of weapons and equipment, but first on mental fortitude, fanatical perseverance, and unshakable belief in the idea and in victory."[100] He claimed Germany could defeat the enemy using propaganda; this tool could achieve much if used correctly.

Goebbels relied on his logic and intuition more than on surveys or official analyses. To give German citizens determination and strength, their national obligation had to be stressed to them, to make them focus only on that. "As long as we are determined to fight the enemy at all costs, we will be undefeated, and to us, being undefeated means being victorious," Goebbels wrote in the editorial of the *Das Reich* newspaper in April 1945.[101]

At that time, when German citizens spent many weeks in underground bunkers attempting to save themselves from aerial bombings, Goebbels decided to close all entertainment and leisure venues, and wipe out all the artistic and cultural activity throughout the Reich. In August 1944, Bormann wrote to his wife: "Dr. Goebbels has submitted a proposal today—please do not speak of it—to close all theaters as a first step in transferring the artists to the military industry."[102]

Goebbels did not forget the power of art. Just then, when the military situation was so difficult, the Germans suffering heavy losses and the front lines in growing need of reinforcement, he ordered that thousands of soldiers and sailors be taken out of active service and assigned to act as extras in the epic propaganda film *Kolberg*, which he produced in mid-1944. The cost of the movie production was eight and a half million Reichsmarks, the most expensive production in Germany to that date. He recruited the best professionals to work on the movie: The music was composed by his favorite musician Norbert Schultze (1911-2002). The director was Veit Harlan (1899–1964), who initially refused to enter into this grandiose production saga in the critical situation Germany was in, but eventually conceded.

The movie describes the battle in which the citizens of Kolberg defended their town against the French forces, between April and July 1807. Goebbels hoped that the movie would strengthen German resistance. The movie was rife with dramatic effects, such as 6,000 horses. Goebbels saw it as a will and testament for future generations and hoped to be remembered for it.[103]

He thought of it as a masterpiece and hoped it would be his greatest legacy. He claimed that the movie could provide some answers to the questions of the German people at the time. He gave it an importance that did not fall short of a military campaign.

On April 17, 1945, less than two weeks before the end of the Third Reich, the premier of the movie *Kolberg* took place. "You have given it your all, Maria" is said at the end of the movie. "And it wasn't for nothing. Death and victory are intertwined. That is just the way it is. Greatness always comes from pain." After the movie was screened for the employees of the Ministry of Propaganda, Goebbels gave a speech:

> "Gentlemen, in a hundred years' time they will be showing another fine color film describing the terrible days we are living through. Don't you want to play a part in this film, to be brought back to life in a hundred years' time? Everybody now has

> the chance to choose the part which he will play in the film a hundred years hence. I can assure you it will be a fine and elevating picture. And for the sake of this prospect, it is worth standing fast..."[104]

In the last year of the war, Goebbels and Hitler still believed there was a chance to turn its tide in Germany's favor. Hitler still relied on the Wehrmacht. He believed they should wait for the right opportunity, and when it came, their fate would change. When would it come? That he could not answer.[105] At that time, Hitler spent night and day poring over maps and military diagrams that described the state of the war. He saw the war through the lens of discussions and documents, far from the blood and filth of the battlefield. At times he would suggest military maneuvers and draw them on the maps, with no relation to the real situation at the front.[106] Gerhard Boldt says that Hitler fell into a world of fantasy and could not wake up from it to deal with reality.[107] He even refused to accept reports of the destruction caused by Allied bombings. When Goebbels sent him an album of photographs of destroyed and damaged monuments and famous buildings, Bormann sent the album back with a note saying that the Führer did not wish to be worried with such irrelevant matters.[108] Linge, too, mentions that Hitler would not listen to bad news, unless it could not be ignored.[109] This stubborn refusal to see reality was the main reason for the continuation of the war, and ultimately, the cause of a great disaster for Germany.[110]

Even though the chokehold was tightening around Germany's neck, there were some who refused to face reality. In the beginning of the 1930s, when speaking of the future war, Hitler said: "Even if we do not win, we will drag half a world down while we ourselves fall." One of the Hitler's general staff officers described him in the last days: "Physically, he looked terrible... he lost his sense of balance... his eyes were bloody... he would often drool from the side of his mouth." His lust for cakes became sickly:

"He would lay around in complete apathy, without a single thought in him... [except] cocoa and cake."[111]

Many in Hitler's close circle testified to his difficult condition at the end of the war. Göring said: "To me there are two Hitlers: one who existed until the end of the French war; the other who began with the Russian campaign... the first Hitler... had much charm and goodwill. He was always frank. The second Hitler... was always suspicious, easily upset, and tense. He was distrustful to an extreme degree... particularly in the last year of the war, a human life was not worth much in his eyes."[112]

Goebbels's physical and mental state also deteriorated in those months, even though he still did his work effectively. His nerves began to buckle under the immense pressure and stress he was under. He began feeling weary, ate almost nothing, and smoked more than in the past.[113] Semmler says that he first saw Goebbels lose control when he learned of the bombing of Dresden: "the tears came into his eyes with grief and rage and shock," Goebbels mourned and was angered and shocked. He met Goebbels again twenty minutes later, and he still cried. He seemed a broken man.[114] The bombing of Dresden in February 1945 influenced him to the point that he suggested to Hitler that they execute a few thousand British and American prisoners of war, as retribution. Helmut Heiber argues that Goebbels's motivation in suggesting that was to breach what remaining moral boundaries the Germans still had in relation to the western allies. If the Führer had taken such severe measures, no more boundaries would have remained, and all ways of action would have been open.[115] Goebbels compered the German and Soviet generals in terms of their aspirations for victory, and he stated in his diary: "Our generals are too old and worn out, and they are complete aliens to our National-Socialist ways of thought and behavior. Many of our generals do not even want a National-Socialist victory. Soviet generals, on the other hand, are fanatical adherents of Bolshevism, and so they fight fanatically for its victory".[116]

However, as Hitler sunk deeper into delusions, had trouble functioning, and closed himself underground,[117] Goebbels continued to visit bombed sites and the front, where he raised the spirits of the German soldiers. His spirits were high when he mentioned the difficulties he had to overcome.[118] In a speech to German soldiers in Görlitz, he spoke of the danger Germany was facing: "The enemy is now at the gates of our city... [It] left us no doubt what it will do to us, to our wives, to our children, and even to our grandchildren and their children."[119]

The fear of Bolshevism was always highlighted in Nazi propaganda in order to convince the Germans that victory was their only option. A Bolshevization of Germany meant not only enslavement, but total annihilation of the German people. After the Polish officers' massacre in the forest of Katyn was discovered, Goebbels mentioned it at every opportunity.[120] It was an excellent anti-Bolshevik propaganda that demonstrated Soviet cruelty and proved what awaited Germany if it didn't win the war. On April 14, 1943, Goebbels wrote in his diary: "I gave instructions to make the widest possible use of this propaganda material."[121] Goebbels hoped that the discovery would cause the Western Allies to stop cooperation with the Soviet Union.[122] One of his clerks pointed out that, if he wouldn't stop mentioning it, some might think that the Germans performed the massacre themselves, and Goebbles answered: "No, no my dear, in Katyn it was no doubt the Russians. Our mass graves are located somewhere else."[123]

According to Hitler and Goebbels, the Germans had themselves to blame for the difficult military situation: They were about to lose because they didn't fight with enough strength and determination. The German people abandoned their government and lost their courage.[124] What value is there in a people whose men do not fight even when their wives are raped? He claimed.

But not only the German people were to blame. Not even the Western Allies or the Soviet Union were completely to blame. They were all victims of a conspiracy that had been brewing in Europe for years. Above everything was always International Jewry. That was what brought about the world war. This was its goal as Hitler predicted it in his speech from

January 30, 1939. In his article "The creators of the world's misfortune", which was published in *Das Reich* in January 21, 1945, Goebbels reminded the German people that they must not forget who was behind the war: "One could not understand this war if one did not always keep in mind the fact that International Jewry stands behind all the unnatural forces that our united enemies use to attempt to deceive the world and keep humanity in the dark." Goebbels would have said that International Jewry is the cement that holds the enemy coalition together, despite their different classes, ideologies, and interests. To Goebbels, Capitalism and Bolshevism had the same Jewish roots, as two branches of the same tree, which bears the same fruit in the end. He saw International Jewry using them both, to suppress the people and keep them in their service.[125]

The same article also claimed that "the International Jewry has a ready-made alibi. Just as they claimed before the great reckoning in Germany, they will attempt to look innocent and claim that there had to be a scapegoat and that they were chosen to be that.

However, this will not help them anymore... they will not be able to hide the proof of their historic fault... even using the most sophisticated lies and hypocrisy." According to Semmler, "Goebbels's hatred of the Jews was fanatical. Everything Jewish was to him like a red rag to a bull. The hatred was so strong that he became incapable of recognizing facts when he had to deal with them."[126] Goebbels developed a pathological hatred of Jews and was extremely vehement in anything related to the policy against them: "I certainly won't rest until the capitol of the Reich, at least, has become free of Jews," he wrote in his diary in March, 1943.[127]

Goebbels's diary did not hide the fact that the extermination of the Jews was taking place and that he had a part in it: "Anyone who is in a situation to do so, must kill the Jews as if they were rats. In Germany, thank God, we have already done the decent thing. I hope this will serve as an example to the world."[128] To increase his power and to show his work was fruitful, he asked for an enhanced role in setting policy: "We activated such a radical policy only when it came to the Jewish question. It was justified, and we are enjoying it today. The Jews cannot hurt us anymore. That is despite having been repeatedly told that there is no answer for it, before having dealt with it. It can now be seen that it is possible if one only desires it."[129]

In addition to achieving his anti-Semitic goals, Goebbels saw the extermination as a spur to the radical policy of "Total War," which Germany now had no choice but to follow: "On the matter of the Jewish question, we have gone so far that we cannot go back. This might be a good thing. According to past experience, a movement and people who burned bridges behind them will relentlessly struggle, as per experience, more than those who have ways to retreat... *we have no other goal than victory*."[130]

Against the background of the war, Goebbels demanded that sanctions be placed on the Jews. For instance, he ordered all actors married to Jewish partners to get divorces. The actor Joachim Gottschalk was married to a Jewish woman named Meta Wolff, and they had a son. Goebbels demanded he divorce her, and when the latter refused, Goebbels had her and their son sent to Theresienstadt. Gottschalk insisted on going with them, but Goebbels prevented him from doing so. In November of 1941, the three family members were found dead after committing suicide by inhaling gas.

According to Goebbels's hateful propaganda, there was a need to sacrifice for German victory, as difficult as it may be, and the Jews had been chosen for that, they who had "swarmed Germany" and threatened to assimilate themselves into the pure German blood. Germans who opposed the Nazi policy were also executed. Only through eliminating the "disruptive elements" could Germany be victorious and salvage itself. Even *Michael* talked of "redemption through sacrifice."[131]

Though he advocated exterminating the Jews, it seems that it was not easy for Goebbels to deal with the situation. Magda told her best friend that her husband had told her horrible things about the Jews: "I am not supposed to talk to anyone about it, and he is placing that burden on me. It is too much, even for him," she said.[132]

And so, in the last year of the war, while millions of Germans were in bunkers, Goebbels found time to write a new book. He wanted to call it *The Virtue of Steadfastness,* but eventually decided to give it the more powerful title, *The Law of War*. Curt Riess mentions that it was a typical Goebbels move—even when he knew the days of the Third Reich were numbered, he wasted his time on this project.[133] But this literary venture can also be seen from a different direction: the worse Germany's condition became, the more Goebbels wanted to keep being active and do something useful and meaningful to him, such as writing a book. This in contrast to Hitler, who simply went from bad to worse.

In the harsh and "constantly hysterical" atmosphere in the bunker, Goebbels remained the calmest person.[134] At the end of April 1945 he still attempted to encourage his team members to keep on with their work. He published his own "Defense Orders." Every Monday, he assembled a "Great War Council," which was attended by military commanders, SS officers, and the mayor of Berlin.

He dispatched hunting squads into the streets, qualified to scan offices and factories in search of men fit to be drafted for war. He ordered posters to be hung on doors declaring that, under the Führer's command, all men aged 15 to 70 were obligated to report for military service. "The cowards that will escape to the shelters... will be court-martialed and executed." And indeed, mobile court martials were established, and they got rid of people who were considered "traitors of the homeland" on the spot, by hanging or shooting.

At that time, Hitler and Goebbels were still contemplating the roles they themselves would play on the stage of history. Goebbels told Hitler that he could still save himself and escape Berlin, to which Hitler responded: "Herr Doctor, you know what my final decision is. It shall remain this way! You are, of course, allowed to leave Berlin with your family." Goebbels replied proudly that he would not do so.

He too, would remain in Berlin and die there. In all the discussions about defending Berlin, the gauleiter stressed that he alone was responsible for the protection of the city.

Hitler's despair was seen in the meeting on April 22, 1945, when it was reported that the Russians had arrived at the northern suburbs of Berlin. Hitler broke down. He screamed that his generals had betrayed him and accused them of cowardice and insubordination. He decided to stay with the Berliners and lead the battle himself when the Russians came. It was then that he admitted for the first time: "It is all over. The war is lost. I shall shoot myself." After that meeting, Hitler offered that Goebbels and his family move to his bunker.[135]

Hitler's bunker contained about twenty small rooms. A corridor led to Hitler's personal quarters. Next to it was a boardroom, where they would hold the status reports. Joseph and Magda made the decision to move to the bunker together. Magda herself decided to commit suicide and take her children with her. "We shall all die," she told her friend, "but by our own hands, not at those of the enemy..." Life after the war would not be worth living. But her husband still affected the decision: "The life that you will all live after the collapse will not be worth living... Suppose I remain alive, I should immediately be arrested and interrogated about Joseph. If I tell the truth, I must reveal what kind of man he was... then any respectable person would turn from me in disgust."[136] She also said that she wanted to spare her children the knowledge of the terrible crimes their father had committed.[137]

Magda and the children moved to Hitler's bunker on the evening of April 19, 1945. She told her children that Uncle Hitler's fifty-sixth birthday was the following day, and they had to congratulate him.

According to Ebermayer and Meissner, Magda was, in a sense, her husband's creation. For years he had trained her to fulfill the tragic role she was given at the end of the war.[138] Manvell and Fraenkel, on the other hand, believe that Magda decided to die with her husband not because she loved him, but to prove she was not any less faithful to the Führer than he was.[139] According to Boldt, Goebbels was in a worse mental state than the others, who stayed in the bunker and whose families were somewhere safe.[140]

Goebbels's decision to commit suicide was a personal one. As a person who had had a full life and a glorious career, Goebbels did not want to end in prison, at the enemy's mercy. He would rather die a heroic death, as he so often preached. He must take part in the last scene in the history of the Third Reich. His death was his first concern. Through his death he could remain a hero in German memory. Now, all that remained was to decide how he would direct the last scene of the *Götterdämmerung*, the "Twilight of the Gods," in order to exit the stage in the most impressive manner.

They had played the Funeral Waltz from *Der Götterdämmerung* many years earlier, at the funeral of Horst Wessel—a member of the SA who was murdered by a communist on February 23, 1930, and was made by Goebbels into the party's martyr and a paragon of Nazi values.[141]

It is also possible that Goebbels himself wanted to step off the stage of history as a fallen god. He was still contemplating how he would exit this world, even during the final days. "Goebbels is not quite certain how his death should happen." Semmler writes, "At one time he talks of suicide at the last moment; at another he plays with the idea of blowing up the shelter, with all of us in it, in the final stages of the battle. Then he will let his imagination play with the picture of himself, swastika banner in hand, dying a hero's death on the barricades."[142]

In a letter he wrote to his stepson Harald Quandt, three days before his family's suicide, Goebbels mentioned that he had asked to be used as an example for the German people in death, of determination in the face of doom. He also noted this in the appendix to Hitler's political testament, the day before his suicide.

Still, while Goebbels was determined to end his life, it seems that Hitler was not keen on committing suicide. If that was the case, then it was Goebbels who influenced his final decision. On Hitler's 56 birthday, April 20, 1945, many of his peers and advisors came to congratulate him at his bunker. Everyone except for Goebbels advised him to leave Berlin. Hitler was pondering it.[143] Goebbels, the master propagandist who knew just how to direct reality to his purposes, controlled the myth of the Führer even in his last moments. In this context, the ending line of his early book, *Michael*, is a prophecy he fulfilled 16 years later: "Many die too late and some early." He wrote, "Still sounds strange doctrine: Die at the right time!"[144]

And so, since they first met, the fates of Goebbels and Hitler were intertwined. Goebbels helped Hitler claim leadership and achieve greatness. This may have only been the prelude to their greatest victory—defeat.[145] Hitler himself said that Germany's greatest tragedy was that it did not have enough time.[146]

The last year of the war was also the last year of the life of Joseph Goebbels, his wife Magda, and their six children. His beloved Führer, to whom Goebbels gave his life, also committed suicide, and Germany lost the war. However, it was also the year in which he was able to reach the height of his power and political influence, after many efforts and much hard work. The crippled, scrawny, awkward boy from a little town in the Rhineland, who was picked on and humiliated throughout his entire childhood and was never able to fulfill his intellectual and artistic vision as an acclaimed writer, reached the height of his aspirations as an influential propagandist, charismatic speaker, and first-class politician.

During that year, Goebbels took a central place in the Nazi regime. Even during that critical year, overshadowed by the imminent defeat and the decline in power of the Nazi regime, Goebbels continued his efforts to make German propaganda an art form, and in doing so, affected the lives of millions of people.

CHAPTER TWO

Nazi Propaganda in the Face of Doom

In 1622, Pope Gregory XV established a church-oriented institute called the Sacred Congregation for the Propagation of the Faith (Sancta Congregatio de Proäpaganda Fide). That was the first official institute to carry the title "Propaganda" and was about spreading the Catholic religion.

Propaganda is not just the art of changing people's opinions and approaches, but also an important tool in strengthening, focalizing, and enhancing existing ones. When it comes to totalitarian regimes, the role of the propagandist is to insert the ideology of the leadership deep into the consciousness of the masses and make them act on it. "There is not much point in discussing propaganda; it is not a theoretical thing, but practical," Goebbels claimed. "'A propagandist of theories' is completely useless; they come up with various methods while sitting at their desks but eventually are amazed and embarrassed when their methods do not serve 'actual propagandists,' or when having to apply them they do not achieve the desired goal."[147]

At the end of World War I, a consensus formed around the premise that the anti-German propaganda deployed by the Allies during the war was a major factor in their victory and contributed to the defeat of Germany.[148] The term *psychological warfare* was coined in the "Great War." The main goal of Nazi propaganda, which Goebbels began developing back in the 1920s, was to create a public consensus around the ideology and policy of the Nazi party. This was the case before the party came to power and was even more so after it did. That goal was validated when the war broke out. Another goal of the propaganda, which was just as important, was keeping the morale of the German people as high as possible, strengthening it during the war and guaranteeing the citizens' loyalty to the regime.[149] The main means for achieving these goals was total control over the flow of information to the greater public.

The foundation upon which propaganda relies is the use of language, both written and spoken. Victor Klemperer, a Holocaust survivor who was in Dresden during the war and who wrote a diary which became well known, developed a theory that had to do with the *language of the Third Reich*, which he called "*Lingua Tertii Imperii.*" He claimed that the most efficient tool Nazism had was not the speeches or articles Hitler and Goebbels wrote, which were often dull and lacked credibility, but Reich's leaders use of *language*. The language in Nazi Germany was no longer autonomous and was subject to the ruling political authority. The repetition of certain words and expressions were forced upon the German public from the top. the meaning of the *word* changed, and it changed from being independent to serving the Nazi system. And so, for instance, the word *fanatic*, which implies extremism and in the most extreme examples is associated with blindness (a blind fanatic), took on a positive meaning in the Reich: Nazism itself was founded on the value of fanaticism and trained all citizens to be fanatic as long as it existed. According to Klemperer, this title—fanatic—was nothing but an inflation of terms such as bravery, dedication, and perseverance.[150] After a letter he sent to an acquaintance returned with a note attached saying that the addressee had "left," he wrote down: "Note to 'The Language of the Third Reich': 'left' means she was forced to do so. It is an innocent word for 'coercion,' 'deportation,' 'sent to one's death.'"[151]

Another characteristic of the language of the Nazi regime was *exaggeration*. For example: the broad use of terms such as *total* and *historical*. Ernst Gombrich claims that, while Nazi propaganda was characterized by its use of lies, it tended to use exaggeration and paranoid formulas more often to describe events.[152]

As far back as the nineteenth century, French polymath Gustav le Bon (1841–1931) claimed that the power of words is so great that even the most despicable phrases become acceptable to the masses upon the propagandist's intervention. Propaganda has the power to change the meaning of words without damaging them. In his very influential *Psychology of the Masses* (*La Psychologie des Foules*), published in 1895, le Bon emphasized the power of the "psychological mass," and that the incredible thing about it was that "no matter the individuals composing it, whether their lifestyles are similar or not... they have a collective soul as a mass, which makes them feel, think, and act differently from how they may have felt, thought, and acted if they had stood on their own."[153]

Similarly, "Frankfurt School" philosopher Theodor W. Adorno claimed that the role of the propagandist is to make people into a mob, meaning "masses eager to perform acts of violence without a reasonable political goal and create a riotous atmosphere."[154] According to Elias Canetti, one of the stand-out characteristics of the mob is its need for direction and guidance, and it exists as long as it has a goal yet to be achieved.[155] William McDougall also claims in his book, *The Group Mind*, that a mob is "extreme in action, displaying only the coarser emotions and the less refined sentiments... incapable of all but the simplest and imperfect forms of reasoning, easily swayed and led, lacking in self-consciousness, devoid of self-respect and of a sense of responsibility, and apt to be carried away by the consciousness of its own force, so that it tends to produce all the manifestations we have learned to expect of any irresponsible and absolute power." He added that "in the worst cases, it is like that of a wild beast, rather than like that of human beings."[156]

An extremely important characteristic of an ideological, regime-based totalitarian country is the government's complete control over its citizens' lives. This includes not only control of individuals' communication with the outside and everything they see, hear, and read, but a complete penetration into their inner lives and control of their beliefs and thoughts. In this regard, the objective of propaganda is to instill certain ideas in a person so that he believes them to be ultimate truth, and feels it is his duty to create an environment that contains and sustains that truth.[157]

One of the fascinating aspects of the Nazi regime was its care not only for the material welfare of its citizens, but also for their mental-spiritual condition, in accordance with the views of Hitler and the Nazi ideologists, of course. The Reich Ministry of Public Enlightenment and Propaganda (*Reichsministerium für Volksaufklärung und Propaganda-RMVP*, or, as it was commonly known, *Promi*), played an important role in that regard. It was established on March 13, 1933, under an order signed by Paul von Hindenburg and Hitler. The official description of the office was "to spread enlightenment and propaganda among the population regarding the policies of the Reich's government and the national construction of the

German homeland." Hitler appointed the thirty-five-year-old Joseph Goebbels to head the office that very day and put him in charge of the "spiritual guidance of the German nation."

As he was appointed, Goebbels wrote in his diary: "I accept under my patronage schools, universities, films, radio, theatre, propaganda. A huge field; an historic mission; I am glad... that the national education of the German people is now in my hands. I will be in control of it."[158] And indeed, Goebbels was the person who brought the art of propaganda to new heights and to dimensions never before seen. In a speech he gave three days after assuming the new position, he said: "I see the establishment of the new office for Enlightenment of the People and Propaganda as a revolutionary act by the government, proving that it has no intention of abandoning its citizens... this government is a government of the people, in the truest sense of the word."

The authority of Goebbels' office was vast: he controlled journalism and radio, events and national holidays, censorship, theatre, books, and films. He was also responsible for advertisement.[159] From the outbreak of World War II until its last few days, almost every morning and at set times, Goebbels would gather his senior employees for ministerial meetings at the office. These meetings were a sort of supervision for Nazi wartime propaganda. Willi Boelcke, who edited and published the protocols of these meetings, states that the way they were run matched Goebbels's character: to him, they were "the height of his day," as he was given a chance to feel self-important. He would not hold consultations, decided everything on his own, and gave instructions.[160]

One of the rising stars of Nazi journalism, Hans Schwarz van Berk, described a typical workday at the Ministry of Propaganda: "The room is empty once or twice a week, and Dr. Goebbels walks around the table. He dictates an article or speech. This happens in the middle of a workday and is mostly so quick that the people in the waiting room are surprised the stenographer already left fifteen minutes later. There were days of such tension and concentration that he would dictate a three-page article in twelve minutes...

when Dr. Goebbels debates, he does so in such a way only few other people can match. He dictates summarized and precise paragraphs, along with some that are elegant and powerful. He does not need much preparation. As a revolutionary, he knows all forms of political expression. That is why, when reading many of his articles, one gets the feeling that he is in fact speaking to them. Articles that have to do with daily issues and foreign affairs somewhat differ—they are written with the appropriate thoroughness. Files and testimonies are collected, quotes are checked in comparison to the originals... after the manuscript has been reviewed several times, it is possible that it will be set aside for a week or more. Then each word is carefully reconsidered... very few people know he [Goebbels] has a very strict daily routine."[161]

Hans Schwarz van Berk was one of the most efficient, professional, and brilliant reporters in the Third Reich. When the war erupted, he was a field reporter and covered the actions of the Waffen-SS in Poland, France, Greece, and the USSR. He supported Nazism and avoided criticizing the Reich's policy, however he attempted to maintain journalistic objectivity and tell the facts as he saw them. During the war he wrote mostly for *Das Reich* newspaper. He gathered a vast readership that appreciated his humane style of writing. An example of that can be seen in the article he sent from the front as Germany invaded the USSR: "We have had a wild night, but Bolshevism would not diminish, who can be surprised? Where is the enemy? Where is the comrade?"[162]

And as Schwarz van Berk described his boss, Goebbels was extremely diligent in his work. He would always wait for the next day, the meetings, the phone calls, the anxiety and concerns, the restlessness and tension that were his position. It seems that this quality of his was what made him so uncompromising in his opinions and his political radicalism. To him, *every problem had a total solution*. He would always over-accentuate the importance of his work in order to elevate his importance as a person. He saw propaganda as an art and himself as the gifted artist who could strum the people's feelings. "Can we diminish the importance of propaganda?" Goebbels once asked in one of his speeches. "Is propaganda, as we understand it, nothing but a form of art? And has that form of art not served the German people greatly over the last fifteen years? Did a National-Socialist party rise to power thanks to ideologists more than propagandists? What would this movement have become if it weren't for propaganda?"[163] He believed that propaganda provided Nazism with its spiritual identity.

According to Werner Stephan, who was an employee of the Ministry of Propaganda and one of Goebbels's first biographers, Goebbels was considered a student who had surpassed his master, Hitler, in his talent for propaganda.[164] Curt Riess said that no one in Nazi Germany knew how the German people thought and felt better than did the Minister of Propaganda.[165] Among other things, his brilliance was in understanding the German psyche, the thoughts and emotional processes of his people. He sought to subordinate all of the public media to the party and make sure that Nazism would have a monopoly over German public opinion. The control over information, under his supervision, was historically unprecedented.[166] As part of his ambition to control all information reaching German citizens, the Ministry of Propaganda acted through various channels: journalism, radio, culture and cinema, active propaganda, word-of-mouth propaganda, and propaganda inside the army.

Journalism

Goebbels compared journalism to a piano—one which the government plays to convey its sounds to the general public.[167] When Hitler rose to power, there were more than 4,700 newspapers in Germany, many of whose writers and owners were Jewish. A year later, in 1934, the Nazi party had complete control over journalism, sometimes directly and other times indirectly.[168] It was then Goebbels's role to replace the Jewish journalists with talented non-Jewish counterparts, which as he admitted himself was quite a task: "Very few flames burn around Germany, the others only reflect their light. It is worse when it comes to the newspapers: we have the best speakers in the world, but we lack agile and talented writers."[169] During the war, Goebbels described the role of the German journalist as "not a regular reporter, but a soldier. Along with guns and grenades, he holds other weapons: a film camera, a Leica, pen or notebook."[170]

The Nazi party purchased the nationalist-extremist newspaper *Der Völkischer Beobachter* as their voice. The newspaper was established in 1920 and contributed considerably to the creation of an anti-Semitic atmosphere in Germany. Its secondary title was "the struggle pages of the National-Socialist movement of Great Germany." Among its prominent writers were Dietrich Eckart, Alfred Rosenberg, and Wilhelm Weiss, who was also the director of the Reich's Association of German Press.[171]

Goebbels himself was responsible for developing journalism in the Reich. He had accumulated journalistic experience even before he was appointed Minister of Propaganda. As early as July 1927, he founded *Der Angriff* newspaper in Berlin. In the pages of the Angriff (literally translated as “the Attack”), he declared that he was challenging the system of the Weimar Republic, and deliberately preached anti-Semitism. The newspaper’s motto was “For the oppressed! Against the exploiters!” According to the Angriff’s editorials, the Weimar Republic was responsible for all the evils experienced by Germany, since it was being run by the traitors who had left the dying soldiers of World War I behind. The rulers of the Weimar Republic were self-interested, and corruption was rooted within the system. Goebbels explained the reasons for those things clearly: it was all controlled by the Jews.[172]

In an article he wrote on July 4, 1927, headlined “Why attack?” (*Warum Angriff?*), he asked: “Have two million of our fathers and brothers fallen at their posts underneath the skies for a different Germany, for the Jews and their German hangmen servants to now make belts of our skins?... to expel the enemies of Germany, the attacker will always be stronger than the defender! That is why we attack!”[173] The Angriff attempted to point the political views of its readership towards Nazism, as well as their opinions on foreign policy, the economy, and internal affairs. It also advocated on matters of the woman's role in the household, raising children, literature, music, and even sports.[174] Historian Karl Dietrich Bracher wrote that by establishing the newspaper, "Goebbels commenced a new era of propaganda, in which ideological casuistry was combined with addressing the masses in the style of Bolivarian newspapers, an effective mixture of defamation and sentimental pathos."[175]

Goebbels also used the services of cartoonist Hans Schweitzer (1901–1980) in the newspapers. Schweitzer would draw heroic warrior characters as "Nazi-like," opposed by ridiculous and despicable caricatures of Jews.[176] Schweitzer was born in Berlin and joined the Nazi party in 1926. His political caricatures made him famous. He became a close friend of Goebbels, and they spent a lot of time together.

Another important newspaper Goebbels edited and wrote editorials for was the weekly paper *Das Reich*, which first saw light in May 1940. According to

Norbert Frei and Johannes Schmitz, Das Reich was the best creation of Nazi journalism. It provided its readers with articles on political and economic topics, and reported from the fronts alongside literary and cultural reviews. Goebbels did not give up on the newspaper's culture section, which throughout the war continued to publish poems, short stories, and literary reviews.[177] For instance, on October 8, 1944, it published an article to mark 100 years since the birth of the philosopher Friedrich Nietzsche. The article stated that one of Nietzsche's main goals was to educate the Germans on a great ideological war that would occur in the twentieth century.[178] Even in the last stage of the war, the Das Reich was a goldmine of information on many topics.

DAS REICH

Nr. 53 JAHR 1944 · DEUTSCHE WOCHENZEITUNG · BERLIN 31. DEZEMBER

DER MANN, DEM WIR VERTRAUEN

AUS DEM INHALT

Bob Hannegan

DER FÜHRER

Von Reichsminister Dr. Goebbels

ADOLF HITLER

ZUSAMMENSPIEL IM WESTEN

Front cover of the newspaper
Das Reich from December 31, 1944

The newspaper *Das Schwartze Korps*, edited by Hasso von Wedel, bore the subtitle “The newspaper of the Schutzstaffel (SS) of the National-Socialist party” and “The Reich’s leadership SS journal,” and was full of anti-Semitic articles. It passionately attacked the Catholic church and the “lustful Jew.” Shortly after the Kristallnacht, on November 24, 1938, the newspaper prophesized that the outcomes of recent events would be "the actual and total end of German Jewry, and its complete annihilation," in an article it published called "Jews, What Now?"[179]

The *Der Stürmer*, privately owned by Julius Streicher (1885–1946), had only one goal: to fight the Jews. It reported, in great detail, the Jews' sexual perversions, until even Goebbels himself remarked that the newspaper was "sometimes outright pornographic."[180] Der Stürmer was established in 1923 and reached a circulation of about 400,000 copies by 1944. It encouraged the passing of laws, orders, and undertaking anti-Jewish means, and projected an atmosphere of terror. The newspaper even provided an informing service for its readers as it would publish names and addresses of people who supposedly socialized with Jewish people. In an editorial by Streicher titled "The census of the Jews, a secret revealed," it said in typically venomous language: "As the Jews' control is broken by National-Socialism, the road set for the question of a Jewish census in the future will no longer be relevant. [The Führer] has predicted the world's Jewry will have their own graves dug up, should they lead to the outbreak of another World War: it would not be the non-Jewish part of the world that faced extermination, but by the end of this second World War, those who were until now named Jews will be the ones who will be exterminated."[181]

Front cover of the newspaper
Das Reich from January 31, 1943

DAS REICH

Nr. 5 JAHR 1943 · DEUTSCHE WOCHENZEITUNG · BERLIN 31. JANUAR

STUNDE DER BEWÄHRUNG

UM DAS ERBE EUROPAS

Zehn Jahre Kampf Adolf Hitlers

Von Reichsleiter Alfred Rosenberg

DER BLICK NACH VORNE

Von Reichsminister Dr. Goebbels

The anti-Semitic newspaper Der Stürmer in which the emphasized motto is: "The Jews are our calamity!"

Der Stürmer

Deutsches Wochenblatt zum Kampfe um die Wahrheit

HERAUSGEBER: JULIUS STREICHER

9

1943

Die Mobilmachung des Volkes

Kampf dem Weltfeind

Der Satan

Aus dem Inhalt

Die Juden sind unser Unglück!

Preis 30 Pfennig

Ritualmord-Nummer

Der Stürmer

…tsches Wochenblatt zum Kampfe um die Wahrheit

HERAUSGEBER: JULIUS STREICHER

Nürnberg, im Mai 1934

1934

Jüdischer Mordplan

gegen die nichtjüdische Menschheit aufgedeckt

Das Mördervolk

Judenopfer

Die Juden sind unser Unglück!

The journalist Ernst Hiemer wrote the following in that newspaper: "When will the Jewish problem be removed? Europe is on its way to provide a final solution to this Jewish question. Precisely for that reason, it would be better to learn from past mistakes... Judaism is an organized crime. That is why the only way to completely remove the Jewish danger is when the entire world's Jewry will cease to exist." As the war broke out, Der Stürmer's editorials remained radical towards the Jews, but the newspaper was rather silent as to their mysterious fate and did nothing to report the deportations, the ghettos, or the extermination. And so, during the years of the war, German media wrote nothing about the death camps or the mass shootings in occupied territories. According to historian Jeffery Herf, this omission in the media can be seen as one of the Nazis' greatest accomplishments as a whole, and Goebbels's and Otto Dietrich's (Hitler's press chief) specifically. The German government not only hid the mass murder of a civilian population, including Jews, but also concealed the number of German lives lost in battle. It was important for Goebbels to keep

German morale up and not provide any unwelcome information.[182]

Another tool for managing the masses was the "Reich Journalism Conferences" Goebbels held in Berlin. The first conference was held on May 15, 1933. A day after he was sworn in as a minister, he gathered the journalists and explained to them that, from that point on, the conference's goal would be "something else": the journalists would no longer report what they knew, but the events of the day that the Nazi government believed the public needed to know. They had to make this information clear and useful for people. The writers received daily instructions on how to treat certain issues in the pages of their newspapers.[183]

One of the first decisions Hitler made upon being appointed Chancellor was to place as Director of the Journalism Department of the Ministry of Propaganda Walther Funk (1890–1960), a chubby, porky man with homosexual tendencies who was the editor of *Berliner Börsenzeitung* for ten years, until joining the Nazi party and serving as Hitler's personal economics assistant.[184] "When I met Hitler, I was taken with his extraordinary personality. He was brilliant in his speeches and his ability to quickly grasp issues," Funk said during the Nuremberg trials.[185] At the head of the party's Journalism Department was Otto Dietrich (1897–1952), Hitler's own Press Chief. His main role was to convey the Führer's instructions to the Ministry of Propaganda. There was great rivalry between Dietrich and Goebbels. When Dietrich said that some of his best ideas came to him as he was taking a bath, Goebbels was quick to ask why he did not take baths more often.[186]

Another important character in the field of controlling German journalism was Max Amann (1891–1957). Also associated with Hitler, he was the Director of the Nazi party's publishing company—Franz Eher Verlag—based in Munich with branches in Berlin and Vienna. Goebbels, Amann and Dietrich would frequently make appointments to coordinate their actions, but these were never realized after their very first meeting was cut extremely short due to their difference of opinions.

Goebbels always made sure that his subordinates did not take too much control over the Ministry of Propaganda. For instance, he insisted that every manuscript to be published by the party had to have his approval. Dietrich, who was appointed the Director of the Reich's Journalism Department in 1937, remained at this influential position until March of 1945. Only then did Goebbels succeed in firing him, after years of rivalry and hostility. One of the outcomes of this rivalry was the fact Goebbels increased the political use of radio, at the expense of newspapers.

Radio

Since 1925, the radio broadcast system was under national supervision via the Reich's Radio Company (Reichsrundfunkgesellschaft), but it did not have control over the broadcast content. From the moment he was appointed, Goebbels understood the potential looming in the radio as a device for propaganda—indeed, it was the most important tool for that purpose. "The radio will be for the twentieth century what journalism was for the nineteenth," he said. Goebbels claimed that the citizens could be brought closer to the leadership via radio broadcasts, creating unified public opinion and guiding the German people to accept the idea of the "people's community." Goebbels appointed Hans Fritsche (1900–1953) as Director of the Radio Department in 1942.[187] Goebbels was aware of the fact that people would listen to the radio for relaxing music as well as catching up on the news. Hitler's speeches would frequently be broadcast on the radio, with each being considered an historic event that could determine the fate of the nation and the world. His speeches were directed by experts, his hysterical and frightening screams well planned. The speeches reached dozens of millions of listeners who felt as if they were themselves part of history in the making.[188] Goebbels's annual speech for Hitler's birthday was broadcast on the radio with music from Wagner's *Die Meistersinger von Nürnberg,* playing in the background.[189] Goebbels thought the radio was the most important and modern means of communication at his disposal. Due to political conflicts, he had with various media managers, the radio became a tool under his complete control, which was why he invested so much in its development.

Culture and Cinema

The Nazi regime methodically organized the cultural lives of the German public and completely controlled them. As the party rose to power, Goebbels assumed control over culture in Germany, and as early as 1933, he established the Reich's Chamber of Culture (Reichskulturkammer). The chamber was in charge of controlling artistic activity according to the regime's policy. According to him, after coming to power the Nazis had to take care of the "cultural chaos" that surrounded the Weimar Republic. The connection between the arts and politics in Nazi Germany was well evident, for instance in the operation to confiscate the "degenerate" art the Nazis carried out in 1937. Culture was the first field to massively expel the Jews.[190] The Kulturpolitik was an important component in German tradition, even before the

Nazis assumed power. The national circles took it on as an expression of the supremacy of the Aryan race over other, inferior people, mostly the Jews.[191] An example of the roots of this idea and concern for the future existence of German culture can be seen in a letter Martin Bormann wrote to his wife towards the end of the war: "Anyone who still believes we have a chance is a great optimist! And that is exactly what we are! I simply cannot believe that fate has placed our Führer and our great nation on this path only to now leave us and see us disappear forever... this means the destruction of everything the culture and civilization ever created. Instead of *Die Meistersinger* we would have to see Jazz shows."[192]

Music was also under the supervision of the Ministry of Propaganda. The composer Richard Strauss (1846–1949) was appointed Director of the Music Chamber (Reichsmusikkammer). In 1935, the Gestapo found a letter of support from Strauss to his friend, Jewish author Stefan Zweig. Following that, Strauss was fired from his position. "It is disgusting that he would write to a Jew," Goebbels commented.

In 1927, journalism mogul and head of the Nationalist right-wing party DNVP—Deutschnationale Volkspartei—Alfred Hugenberg (1856–1951), nicknamed the "Press Czar" ("Pressezar"), purchased the most esteemed film company in Germany at the time, Universum Film AG (UFA). Following that move, the activity of the Nazi party became ever more accessible to the German public by the screening of more and more propaganda films. Goebbels's office was in charge of producing a variety of films: features, documentaries, shorts, etc. The Reich's Film Chamber was established immediately following the Nazis' seizure of power and was headed by Carl Froelich. Both Hitler and Goebbels loved this medium and would watch many movies and discuss them. They claimed that the Jews controlled the American film industry and feared it would influence the German one. That is why, starting from July 1933, they began the "Aryanization" of the film industry and its subjection to the Reich's purposes. There was special supervision on scripts and their writers.[193] Between 1933–1945 there were 1,086 films produced in Germany, with only a small part of them categorized as strictly propaganda. About half of them were romantic films or comedies, a quarter of them were thrillers or musicals. This points to the importance Goebbels attributed to the entertainment of the masses during the war. At the beginning of 1941 he said that, in order to lead a war, the people must be kept in high spirits, and this could be achieved through culture and entertainment.

After the events of the Kristallnacht, in November 1938, Goebbels gave a speech in which he presented Germany's position and justified the riots which he himself had a lot to do with.[194] The Jews had to feel the wrath of the people, he said. Following the riots, the Gestapo arrested about thirty thousand Jewish men who were sent to the Dachau, Buchenwald, and Sachsenhausen concentration camps. Following criticism on the matter, Goebbels realized that not all Germans were "enlightened" enough on the subject of the "Jewish threat." He recruited his favorite medium, film, and came up with the idea of producing a movie about the Jews which he referred to as a "documentary." He chose a distinct, well known, and popular motif to serve as the movie's title: *The Eternal Jew* (*Der ewige Jude*),[195] through which he attempted to convey the message that the Jews were responsible for everything that was bad in the German society. *The Eternal Jew* was written by Eberhard Taeubert (1907–1976), lawyer by trade, who was the head of the Jewish Affairs division of the Ministry of Propaganda. It was set in Germany in 1542 and became a very powerful tool in the mythological applications that called out for the destruction of Judaism. The wandering Jew was the one who mocked cross-bearing Jesus on his way to Golgotha and was therefore cursed by Jesus to eternally wander and have a joyless life, *which only death would redeem on Judgment Day*. According to anti-Semitic sources, the wandering Jew was evil and damaged the Germans, as he gave them cholera and syphilis and became the Jew that was to be blamed for all the world's woes. However, this Jew did not become a representation of a single character, but rather carried within him a collective guilt rooted in nationless Judaism. Every Jewish person, wherever he may be, carried that curse with it. The script sought to provide a scientific explanation of the inferiority of the Jews and justify the anti-Semitic policy the country had taken against them. The movie shows the Jews as a parasitic race that damages humanity and therefore must be exterminated. The movie, directed by Fritz Hippler (1909–2002), was reedited and altered, becoming crueler and more bloodthirsty each time. "Each time the rats appear, they bring more destruction to the land," the voiceover said. "They destroy men's property and food. They spread diseases and leprosy, typhoid, cholera, and dysentery... they are not much different from the Jews." In addition to *The Eternal Jew*, Goebbels personally oversaw the production of two other anti-Semitic films: *Die Rotschilds* (*The Rothchilds*) and *Jud Süß*, which was based on a book by Lion Feuchtwanger about the Jew Joseph Süß Oppenheimer, who was sentenced to death for embezzlement. Goebbels added to the main character, a greedy Jew who attempted to force himself on German society in the eighteenth century, the sexual assault of a blond girl—the perfect Aryan woman—who commits suicide following the rape. The end of the Jewish villain was death by hanging in the town square. The film, released in 1940, was very successful and became a hit. Himmler issued an order that instructed the SS soldiers to watch it.

Another important figure in the Nazi film industry was the director and photographer Leni Riefenstahl (1902–2003). Her documentary *Triumph of the Will* (*Triumph des Willens*) in 1934 expressed the power of the Nazi party and especially Hitler as a strong leader of his people. Her relationship with Goebbels was often tense and he described her as "hysterical," claiming that "one cannot work with such wild women... she cries. It is the women's last weapon. But that does not work on me anymore. She'd better work and keep order."[196]

Active Propaganda

A main department in the Ministry of Propaganda was "Active Propaganda," initiating a variety of activities around Germany. For example, from 1936, the official public posters of the Nazi party, the weekly "wall newspaper" *Word of the Week* (*Parole der Woche*), were circulated every Thursday.[197] This was the most invasive and extensive tool of visual propaganda of Nazi Germany. The posters, hung in public places and visible to people who passed by them on the streets, had texts and images that conveyed the messages the regime sought to promote. The posters, conquering the public space, had extreme anti-Semitic messages.

Another role of the Active Propaganda department was planning and executing public events, such as Party Day in Nuremberg, mass parades, and smaller gatherings in smaller towns. The department gave directions to the people speaking at those conventions. Visuals played an important role in Goebbels's propaganda and included motifs such as uniforms, flags, and symbols. The department issued its own periodical called *Our Will and Way* (*Unser Wille und Weg*). The Ministry of Propaganda also supported the activity of various nationalist associations that could advance its goals. For instance, the Fichte-bund, established in 1914 by Heinrich Kessemeier, spread racial and pan-Germanic propaganda. Among the first members of this association was the aforementioned publicist Dietrich Eckart (1868–1923), Hitler's own mentor.

Word-of-Mouth Propaganda

One of Goebbels's favorite techniques was word-of-mouth propaganda, a method in which rumors were spread throughout the populace using imposters or in random staged conversations. These rumors were meant to prepare the public for what was about to take place. This was a form of psychological warfare. For instance, before the German invasion of the USSR, the regime seeded clues to that possibility. The technique was well known and was not invented by the Nazis, but it had never been used so extensively as it was under Goebbels.

Propaganda in the Military

Special emphasis was placed on propaganda among German army personnel, the Wehrmacht. A special propaganda unit (Wehrmachtpropaganda Abteilung) operated inside the army and had a Waffen-SS unit subject to it. Its role was to maintain Nazi ideology within the army and instill it into the various corps. The Air Force, Navy, and ground corps constantly reported to these units, a process which became harder as the war grew longer. There was always a military press officer at the head propaganda office, and there were naturally conflicts and disagreements between the military and civil personnel, mostly surrounding the way propaganda in the military was organized and supervised. The unit also spread anti-Semitic and anti-Partisan propaganda in conquered areas. Following the invasion of Poland in September 1939, the Ministry of Propaganda requested that the army's propaganda units transfer to Berlin photographs of Jews for the purpose of anti-Semitic "explanation." And so, in October 1939, the following message was sent to the front after the occupation of Warsaw: "We should procure a larger amount than we had until now, from Warsaw and all the occupied territories, film sections displaying different types of Jews. Portraits of Jews and Jews working are preferable. This material is meant to strengthen our anti-Semitic propaganda in the country and around the world."[198] The photos of the Jews were meant to display the "Jewish stereotype," and they were used, for instance, in the venomous propaganda movie *The Eternal Jew.* A propaganda branch of the Wehrmacht was in charge of the ideological education of soldiers and screened anti-Semitic movies in the different units. It was especially important to explain to the soldiers, after the invasion of the USSR, that the Jews were controlling the Bolshevik system and were taking advantage of it.

Goebbels constantly followed the state of Germany's military and the state of the German people's morale.

The SD's reports on the population's morale, which were classified as top secret, were routinely provided to him, but they were insufficient. His office's team would directly speak to clerks, citizens, and soldiers, and learned from them firsthand. Goebbels did not rely on surveys or analysis made by others and preferred his own intuition, judgment, and experience.[199] He believed he had to know the truth about what was happening, and the reason was, as he attested to himself: "How can I present the status of things, if I do not know where people can be deceived?"[200]

The Reich's citizens were subject to a ban on any foreign newspapers, listening to the radio, or having any other contact with the Allied forces, and the Ministry of Propaganda was "holier than the Pope" in respect to this. Goebbels's office knew the enemy's propaganda and, according to van Berk, "the most important thing to follow is the enemy. We cannot afford trench fighting in propaganda [meaning, being static]. Every issue of the enemy must be immediately replied to."[201] To Goebbels, the various propaganda departments were as members of a great symphonic orchestra that he was conducting, as they responded to all his instructions in a unique and sophisticated style.[202]

Nazi propaganda was unique in its merging of the practical and political with the mystical and its merging matters of traditional German patriotism with ideological Nazi motifs. Goebbels maintained a few basic principles that helped him and his methods succeed: one must approach the people's instincts and feelings; one must try and use the most primitive arguments and the most popular phrases in order to ensure the masses understand its ideas; one should not tell uncomfortable facts; one must repeat the same ideas and slogans, over and over again, so even the stupidest person will remember them; one must repeat lies until they are accepted as truths. The sole purpose of propaganda is to succeed. All means justify the cause. Goebbels emphasized that the value of the propaganda campaign depended only on the reply to the question: Did it work?[203]

To assure understanding of it, there is often a need to "fill in" more details in the propaganda narrative. In November 1944, Semmler wrote about a new term that had entered Goebbels' vocabulary: "Poetic Truth," meaning "when we know very little about a certain event, we must describe it as it should have occurred. In Goebbels's words, 'we are only helping the public when we call imagination to our aid in certain cases where the record of the facts is for some reason incomplete!". According to him, many events in international politics could not be understood unless one embroidered them a little with the "poetic truth" and so made them understandable to the German public.[204] Goebbels repeatedly stressed the following slogans: "This war was forced on us;" "This war is a matter of life and death;" "We now need the effort of a total war."[205]

The last meeting of the Ministry of Propaganda team led by Goebbels was held by candlelight, since there was no longer electricity at the ministry, and on February 23, 1945, a bomb landed on the ministry's office while Goebbels was away and completely destroyed it. Goebbels went to see the destruction with his own eyes. "It has been twelve years to this day, March 13, since I entered this office as minister; it is an ominous sign for the next twelve years. My entire team is on the scene and attempting to salvage what they can. But there is nothing left to salvage from the most beautiful part of the building," he wrote in his diary.[206] He then transformed his residence on Herman Göring street into an office.

Nazi Propaganda: A Weapon against the Bolsheviks and the Jews

To the Nazis, there were two main enemies of the German people: the Jews and the Slavs (*Slav-Untermenschen*). Goebbels understood that the Germans would have a hard time accepting the fact that they were fighting several fronts simultaneously, against several enemies, and he sought to simplify his propagandist messages at once. Therefore, these two enemies were unified under one category, which he referred to as *Judo-Bolshevism*. In his famous speech after the defeat at Stalingrad, Goebbels stressed the standing of the Jews behind the Allied forces and their influence on the war against the Germans: "Anywhere you look in the enemy camp, there are Jews in the background for inspiration, inciting and lashing them."[207]

To end the war, the Allies demanded from Germany unconditional surrender, a demand which ran against the very basis on which Nazism was established. This situation led Goebbels to create threatening propaganda, depicting the fate awaiting the Germans under Bolshevik rule. He spoke of the danger the "mongoloid Bolshevik-Jews" posed as they sought world domination.

According to him, the Germans faced this danger of the destruction of their civilization all on their own, and ready for battle. The slogan he used often at that time was "Western civilization is in danger." Goebbels posed difficult questions to the German people: did they believe in an ultimate victory and were they willing to follow the Führer in order to accomplish it? Were the Germans ready, from then on, to use all the resources at their disposal and do whatever it took to prevent the death blow? Following

Stalingrad, Nazi propaganda had to walk a tightrope and maintain balance between spreading fear of the Bolsheviks and strengthening faith in the ability of the German people to win. Goebbels declared: "Stalingrad was and still is the greatest warning of the fate of the German people! A people able to bear such disaster and draw power from it is invincible," and once again he stressed the Bolshevik danger, seeking to Bolshevize every foreign country and people on the face of the earth.[208]

Discovering the mass grave in the Katyn forest demonstrated Bolshevik cruelty and the danger of which the Ministry of Propaganda had warned. Goebbels used that massacre often: the entire Reich was awash with threatening slogans against the Bolsheviks such as "Victory or Bolshevism"; "Total war—the shortest war"; "Our Führer will crush the Bolsheviks"; "We should no longer defend—we're moving to offense!" In those days Goebbels also proudly mentioned in his diary that "the Führer completely supports my anti-Bolshevik propaganda. It is the best horse in our stable right now." It was written in the Ministry of Propaganda protocols: "The minister mentions that the anti-Bolshevik campaign has exceeded expectations... the Bolshevik danger was positioned at the forefront of the discussion."[209]

Anti-Jewish propaganda continued alongside anti-Bolshevik propaganda. Even when it came to the murder of the Polish soldiers and officers in Katyn, the "blood libel" of the Jews was stressed and it was said that Jewish officers in the Red Army were those who massacred the Poles.[210]

The order by the German Press Department to add the name "Finkelstein" before the last names of the Jewish Russian leaders, points to the tight relationship between Jews and Bolsheviks that the Nazi regime wanted to depict. And so Russian Minster of Foreign Affairs Maxim Litvinov became Finkelstein-Litvinov in the German press.[211]

In an article titled "The War and the Jews" (*Der Krieg und die Juden*), Goebbels wrote that it was the Jews who ideologically and financially supported the war, and that "our political security demands that we take all necessary means needed to protect the

German people from the threat they oppose... this war is racial. The Jews started it, and they are stirring it. Their goal is to destroy and annihilate our people. We are the last force that stands between the Jews and their goal of ruling the world."[212]

This article served as an example for Nazi propagandists and made such a clamor that it surprised even its author. This is what Goebbels wrote in his diary: "To my great surprise, my article 'The War and the Jews' attracted much attention. I thought that Jews would attempt to overlook it, but that is not the case. It is so widely quoted that it is hard to believe. Which goes to show that the Jews are stupid for publishing my claims around the world, or that there is someone sitting in every editorial position... who opposes the Jews."[213]

In an earlier article, Goebbels outspokenly discussed the punishment that Jews were subjected to under the Nazi regime. Regarding Hitler's prophecy about their fate, he wrote: "We are witnessing the realization of this prophecy. The Jews are being undoubtedly severely punished, but it is more than well deserved... the Jews are our historical enemy." He believed that the Jews sought the surrender and destruction of Germany.[214]

Goebbels's attacks on the Jews served two goals: first, they were made responsible for the war under the thesis of "the great conspiracy," which proposed that International Jewry was behind the Allied leaders. Second, these attacks made the Germans agree with the anti-Jewish steps the regime had taken. The Jews would not escape their Judgment Day, Goebbels said, and repeated the slogan: "The Jews are to blame! The Jews are to blame!"[215]

In an article of that title, Goebbels wrote that "the Jews are a parasitic race... the fact that the Jews still live among us is not proof that they are part of us, just as the flea will not become a pet simply because it is in the house."[216] Other places in Nazi Germany also identified the Jews with harmful biological organisms that had to be expelled so that their German hosts would survive. Hitler wrote in his book, *Mein Kampf*, that a Jew "is and remains a parasite, a sponger who, like a pernicious bacillus, spreads over wider and wider areas accordingly as some favorable area attracts him. The effect produced by his presence is also like that of the vampire; for wherever he establishes himself the people who grant him hospitality are bound to be bled to death sooner or later."[217]

Goebbels chose to describe the actions against the Jews with the word *ausschalten,* which means to expel, turn off, mostly in the phrase *Einfluss ausschalten*—to turn off the influence.[218] As early as 1943, Goebbels was certain he had accomplished one of the greatest political achievements of his career when he exterminated the Berlin Jewry: "When I think of how Berlin looked when I arrived here in 1926 and how it looks today, in 1943, when its Jews are entirely banished, only then can I understand what I have accomplished," he wrote in his diary.[219] At the end of May 1943, Berlin was declared free of Jews (*Judenfrei*), but it was during that time that Goebbels started ever-so-prominently publicizing the fact that Germany was in a war of survival against them, and that they sought nothing less than extermination (*Ausrottung*) of the German people.[220] Goebbels took advantage of the German mothers' and fathers' pressure point—their children's lives: "Every German soldier who fell in this war is registered to the Jews' fault. They are on their conscience, and they should, therefore, pay for it [with their own deaths]."[221] According to him, it made no sense that Jews were still wandering around the Reich's capital. Getting rid of them was the only way to rid Germany of the problem once and for all.

About a year before the end of the war, on March 2, 1944, orders were given at the Ministry of Propaganda: "Now, more than ever, we must stress the issue of anti-Semitism in the propaganda... therefore, we must tarnish International Jewry every chance we get, such that its cunning mechanism conflicts with the interests of the countries in which the Jews live... we must emphasize the true destructive intentions of the Jews..." One of the goals of Nazi propaganda was to take this anti-Semitic dialogue outside the borders of Germany and display Judaism as a global danger. A total war against the Jews was the only alternative to the total destruction of Western civilization.

In a meeting of the department heads of the Ministry of Propaganda on January 4, 1943, Goebbels declared the need to change to a more determined thought process: "I myself would like to see the idea that we are invincible disappear from my mind and yours. We might indeed lose the war. People who do not apply themselves may bring on defeat, while those who put in a lot of effort can bring on triumph. We should not fatally believe in a certain victory; we must think positively... we will easily win this war if we pluck every nerve now. We have all the winning cards... we have to muster all of our power, and this is what we are about to do on a large scale."[222]

Goebbels used the term "Homefront" (*Heimatfront*), which meant treating the homeland as another front. The goal of this was strengthening the unity between the soldiers at the front and the civilians at home. He used this motif in the total war campaign, where he advocated "a struggle on all fronts." The propaganda directed at the German citizens in the rear was meant to cause them to fear the outcomes that losing the war would entail, but without bringing them to complete despair. Confidence and trust in the regime were, according to Goebbels, the most efficient morale weapons in the war. The people would never be closer to their Führer as in times of danger, when the leader needed his supporters as much as they needed him. And indeed, in the last stage of the war, Goebbels acted even more to glorify the image of the Führer, who's mental and health state had started to decline. That was when Goebbels started using the motif of doom (*Untergangsmotif*), which described the war as an ideological struggle between life and death, triumph or termination.[223] Goebbels used the description of the horrors committed by the enemy as a means to increase and strengthen the perseverance of civilians. The enemy would be portrayed cruelly, so—he hoped—that the German people would fight out of greater fear and would not surrender. Hitler also claimed, in his speech before his army's commanders on June 22, 1944, that this war was the decisive battle for the existence of the German people.[224]

As matters worsened, the propaganda adopted the technique of exaggeration to encourage citizens to continue the war effort. For instance, the press, radio, and posters repeatedly used phrases such as: "fanatic effort," "fanatic decisiveness," "fanatic stance." There were occasionally other attributes added to strengthen the fanatic adjective: "Cold fanaticism and hot hate" (*kaltem Fanatismus und heissem Hass*), "Holy fanaticism" (*heiligem Fanatismus*), "Wild fanaticism" (*wildem*), or stubborn (*trotziger*).[225]

Following the surrender of the Sixth Army at Stalingrad, in opposition to Hitler's order to keep fighting to the end, it was Germany's time to face the cataclysmic results. The euphoria of German victories had come to an end, and so did the promise of victory and the prestige of the Wehrmacht as an invincible army. To exert political control of a situation that had turned out to be catastrophic, Goebbels decided to declare three days of mourning in which all theaters, cinemas, and other entertainment venues would be closed. From then on, he commenced a policy of radicalization in Germany, which he hoped would lead to regaining strength, allowing Germany to overcome their materialistic, morale, and mental dire straits. Following that defeat, a distinctive (and rather ironic) trend began in Goebbels's status, which lasted until the end of the war. As his status and power in the regime grew, the power of Germany and its Supreme Leader Hitler declined. In a speech he gave on January 31, 1943, Goebbels warned his audience that "there is only one sin... the cowardice of the heart!" Despite the disaster they endured, the Germans had to overcome it and harden their hearts, he said.[226] And in his famous speech at the Berlin Sportpalast, on February 18, 1943, with a big banner behind him saying "Total War—the shortest war," he once again called for "Total War" and addressed the German people's need for solidarity and facing forward towards the fighting, all the way to victory: "The English claim that the German people opposes the government's plan of total war; do you want total war? Do you want, if need be, for it to be more radical and total than anything we could imagine today? I ask you, are you determined to follow the Führer, and bring the war to a victorious end, even if it means you must bear the greatest of personal burdens?"[227] "The Führer commands—We obey!" The audience cheered. Goebbels continued his speech: "From now on, our slogan will be 'Rise up, and let the storm break loose!'" Goebbels took this last sentence from Theodor Körner, a poet from the time of Prussia's uprising against Napoleon.

Goebbels giving a speech and announcing an economic boycott against Jews, in Berlin, Germany, April 1, 1933. Yad Vashem Photos Archive

Gunther Moltmann claims that Goebbels entered the most important stage of his career following this speech.[228] Thanks to the "art" of propaganda he developed and the articles he published, Goebbels's importance to the Nazi leadership was validated. Until the end of the war and the defeat of Germany, which also brought on the end of Goebbels's career and his life, he served as Hitler's main consultant, immensely influencing the decision-making of the government, and becoming one of the most powerful people in the Nazi regime.

In the last stage of the war, there was a need for myths in order to explain the harsh conditions Germany was facing. For instance, in the film *Kolberg*, Goebbels showed the German people what they must do at that time. He tried to show them that victory was achieved thanks to the citizens and not necessarily thanks to the army. The historical facts show that the people of Kolberg, despite their heroic stance, were finally defeated by the French, but Goebbels decided to overlook this fact. This shows, as David Welch claims, how much the Nazi leadership sank into the mystical world of its creation.[229] The director of the film, Veit Harlan, who was also a famous film actor, said in an interview after the war: "It seemed that Hitler and Goebbels were obsessed with the idea of the film, and believed that its propagandist power would be greater than a military victory in Russia."[230]

Germany's war against the forces of evil, mostly represented by the Jews, was among the dominant myths of Goebbels's propaganda in the last year of the war. The Jewish War (*Der jüdische Krieg*) gave meaning to the hard events that befell Germany.[231] This assault on the Jews gave the propaganda the unity it needed to maintain its influence. Robert J. Lipton wrote of a manipulative world characterized by "ideological totalitarianism." In such a world, there is a clear distinction between pure and impure—absolute good and absolute evil. By using propaganda, the perception is created that all means to achieve the "absolute good" are ethical, in the eyes of the regime, of course.[232] The German people and its leadership were caught up in this web of illusions: if they fought everyone, everyone would fight them, and the less mercy they showed, the more they could rally to fight to the end. There was no way to escape this vicious circle.

In the latter half of the war, parallel to the defeats of the Wehrmacht and the increasing bombardments on German civilians, the promise to make use of new missiles, magical weapons of retaliation (*Vergeltung*), became one of the most important issues in Nazi propaganda.[233] Werner Neumann (1909–1982) was one of the most influential people in that area of propaganda and one of the less conscientious clerks in the Ministry of Propaganda. He asked the Germans to sustain their "perseverance" (*Durchhaltewillen*) until the weapons were activated. At the end of March 1945, he explained: "When the Führer says we will force historical change this year, it is our reality. What does it point to? We do not know. The Führer knows."[234]

This promise was a kind of hope for revenge on the Allies, for the anguish they caused the bombarded population, while giving confidence to the Führer—who still believed in a German victory. Reports from the SD police indicated a harsh and distressed mood among the German population at the time, and a "sense of doom and gloom" (*Untergangsstimmung*) that caused a mental state described as "bombing psychosis." Another report by the SD determined as early as July of 1943 that no one wanted to hear about the *Vergeltung* from Dr. Goebbels anymore! However, their belief in a retaliation action remained their only hope to end the bombardments. Only a deathblow could change the face of the war.[235] The missiles were quickly nicknamed *Versager*—failure. A common phrase that was heard in the streets of the bombarded cities was "A horrible end is better than endless horror."[236]

Most of the citizens in the bombarded cities believed that their situation wouldn't be any worse if the Reich were defeated, since they had nothing left to lose. On the other hand, there were those who still believed there was a chance the tide would turn in Germany's favor, and sought revenge.[237] However, the hopes of a turn in the war failed after the V1 and V2 missiles (the V standing for the retaliation action—

Vergeltung) were launched in mid-July 1944 and did not live up to expectations.

Otto Meissner claims that "the unique weapon Germany really possessed was the mind of its Minister of Propaganda."[238] Goebbels would visit the front frequently and personally met with soldiers and commanders. During one of his visits, he spoke before the soldiers and said they were heroes writing a great chapter in the history of the war via the attack swing (*Angriffschwung*): "There will never come a time when we surrender, and there was never an example, in history, of a people who were defeated without deciding to go to their doom all on their own."[239] After the visit, he wrote in his diary: "Here is a crowd truly willing to accept my views. My speech was only about fighting and resilience," he also wrote that he had found that the soldiers' combat spirit to be great, just as in the good old days. "I strengthened them with a series of convincing historical examples... one can only imagine the volume of influence such a speech has in this kind of an assembly. I feel very happy and serene."[240]

In a desperate attempt to prevent defeat, the Volksstrum units—the "People's Storm"—were established at the end of 1944 for last-ditch resistance. These units were composed of either very young or very old men, since all the rest were at the front. Their main task was to defend Berlin. Jokes quickly emerged regarding those units; their members were described as "men who carry sport-guns and peg-legs."[241] Semmler also wrote in his journal: "The Berlin's Volksstrum units are at the front. They have nothing but guns. Everyone realizes it is insane."[242]

At this time, the *Werwolf*— "wolfman"—movement was established, though it was not turned against the enemies of Germany, but rather against its very own citizens. The role of this partisan movement was to locate and destroy the deserters and traitors to the motherland and sabotage the actions of the Red Army.[243] At the end of the war, the *Werwolf* soldiers added to the atmosphere of fear and terror in the streets of Germany. Their slogan was "Hatred is our prayer; revenge is our battle cry!" And so those who sought to evade getting drafted to fight the Bolsheviks found themselves fighting their own people.

In the final stage of the war, when Hitler was silent in the media, Goebbels kept setting the tone and addressed the German population for the regime. However, at that difficult hour, the civilians were looking to hear Hitler and find in him a source of solace and security. His silence concerned them, and he, for his part, waited for a meaningful military victory in order to make a speech. In a letter to Himmler from Gottlob Berger (1896–1975), a senior member of the Reich's Ministry of Defense, he complained that "Dr. Goebbels is no longer believable… I think the Führer should appear before the people, so that the common man who loyally and bravely fulfills his duty… and remains loyal to him [Hitler] can find refuge from our troubles."[244]

Goebbels maintained two sturdy beliefs until the end of the war: his hatred of Jews and his allegiance

(*Gefolgschaftstreue*) to Hitler. Even several days before their suicide, Goebbels continued to preach to his people resistance at any cost: "The war has come to the point where only the greatest of efforts of the entire nation and every individual alone can save us... all men, women, and children must fight with unparalleled fanaticism... no village or city should surrender to the enemy... as long as we are determined to resist at any cost, we will be undefeated," he later added. "It is the basis of our final victory. This may seem unreasonable now, but it is not so: the final victory shall be ours. We will achieve it with blood and tears, but it will justify all the sacrifices we have made."[245]

Goebbels, who was appointed to head the propaganda and education mechanism of the Third Reich, fulfilled his role by taking over the German masses. The propaganda he spread was actually preaching for destruction—the destruction of the enemies of Germany, which turned into self-destruction in the final stage of the war. He called for the Germans to keep fighting and resisting, maintaining the murderous mechanism against the Jews even when the Germans themselves were lost, and thus making them sink even deeper into their own doom.

CHAPTER THREE

Der Untergang

In the last year of World War II, the Allied attacks on civilian targets in Germany increased, reaching a peak with the bombing of the city of Dresden on February 14, 1945. This bombing killed dozens of thousands of citizens, and the city was almost completely destroyed. From January to April 1945, there were about 471 thousand tons of bombs dropped on civilian and military targets in Germany. Goebbels wrote in his diary, the day after the Würzburg bombing, on the nights of March 17 and 18: "A bleak report has arrived from Würzburg. The recent terror raid on the city destroyed all cultural monuments and 85% of the housing. Würzburg was a city which had hitherto remained immune from enemy air raids. So, the last center of German culture goes down in dust and ashes. If ever we are fortunate enough to have this war behind us, we shall have to begin again from the beginning. There will not be much of the old world left."[246]

On April 20, 1945, Hitler's last birthday, Berlin suffered a fiery blow. The citizens of battered Germany had been forced to endure horrors for the past months, but there was no real attempt within the Führer's bunker to make them stop. This was despite senior leadership acknowledging the public's somber mood, as Martin Bormann wrote to his wife on April 2, 1945: "... the most horrible thing of all is the desperation that grabs hold of everyone—both civilians and soldiers—regarding the feeling that 'there is no use resisting anymore.' I repeatedly drew the attention of the Führer to the destructive effect of the endless air strikes on the morale of the citizens and soldiers." Even Bormann realized that Hitler would not change his policy, and so he went on to write: "We have sworn to fulfill our duties, be it as may. If we are sentenced, as the ancient Nibelungs, to be destroyed... we will march to our death proud and with our heads held high!"[247]

Those quotes by the two people closest to Hitler attest to the atmosphere at the top of Nazi leadership in those fateful days. They realized the harsh situation yet were unwilling to accept the fact that the only outcome for Germany was defeat, and they attempted to find meaning in this catastrophe.

This was also due to the outcome of Nazi propaganda, which accentuated the importance of the Germans' first stance against defeat. Rudolf Höss, the Commander of Auschwitz, wrote in his memoires that, by the end of 1944, it was obvious that all was lost, but Goebbels kept talking about Germany's victory. "Even when I had heavy doubts rising," Höss wrote, "I should have not doubted the final victory. I had to believe it, even though my human common sense explicitly told me that we had to lose that way... no one dared speak of it to his fellow man. It is not because they were afraid to be sentenced for defeatism, but because no one wanted to believe it was true. This could not have been so, to have our world destroyed." That was why his subordinates at the death camp continued their rapid work. Those who slacked off, saying it would not make any difference, were punished.[248]

The person completely blind to the harsh reality, overlooking it completely, was Hitler himself. His fixation on achieving victory in the war and completing his racist goals made the remaining time factor of the war very significant. The stubborn refusal to see reality was, according to Ian Kershaw, the main factor in prolonging the war before Germany's final defeat.[249] After having experienced one, Hitler constantly feared another assassination attempt and was certain those around him were traitors and conspirators. The pressure of time he was under made it difficult to perform political and military calculations. Even when he knew the strategic advantage had shifted towards his enemies, he declined any offer of negotiation and remained adamant about keeping the war going.[250] He was persistent in his way to the very end, as Goebbels testified a few days before the final defeat: "The Führer is tirelessly exhorting the generals to keep resisting and use whatever means necessary to send more battalions to the Western front. He is calling each general individually, almost every day, and clarifying to them what is at stake and what their duties and obligations are." Goebbels thought military actions alone would not be effective and that they had to act to raise morale and strengthen the people: "I believe it would have been better had the Führer addressed the people directly, since that is where the most basic form of resistance lies... the situation is such that only a word from the Führer can lift the emotional crisis that the people now suffer."[251]

Goebbels's propaganda accentuated that, in the nation's darkest hour, citizens must endure the greatest sacrifice: "Germany must live—even if we must die!"[252]

Despite the Allies' bombings and the dire straits, the German people were in, the leadership attempted to maintain the internal unity of the German community, both at the front and at home.

Those who did not fulfill their duty were presented as traitors.[253] German civilians had to come together, to serve as a sort of solace for families who had lost their loved ones, and they knew that during such harsh times, all Germans shared a similar fate and that they were not alone in their sorrow and grief.

In Goebbels's last radio speech, given on April 21, 1945, a day after Hitler's birthday, he addressed the "defenders of Berlin, the eyes of your wives, your mothers, and children are turned to you. They have entrusted their lives, their happiness, health, and future in your hands. You know what the task at hand is, and I know you will see it through professionally. The moment of truth is upon us. I will remain with my team in Berlin. My wife and children are here, as they shall remain. I will do everything within my power to recruit for the defense of the Reich's capital. My thoughts and actions will always be with you, and we will reject our common enemy. We have to stop the Mongol horde at the gates of our city. Our struggle will be the signal for the entire nation to rise up and fight with iron-like decisiveness. Full of a fanatic will to never let the capitol of the Reich fall to the Bolsheviks, we will work and fight together."

Within all that, as the population lay in desperation, fear, and defeatism, Germany had a leadership crisis. Hitler secluded himself, detaching himself from the outside world and drawing himself into a fantasy world. He was depressed and felt that "other than Mrs. [Eva] Braun, no one would agree to live with him of their own will for long..." as Speer recalled.

During those hard times Hitler decided to pursue the dream of his youth and go back to being an artist, an architect who would rebuild his beloved city of Linz, rather than a politician and a leader whose role was to take care of his people's welfare.[254] At Hitler's order, architect Hermann Giesler built a miniature model of the city of Linz. The model was ready on February 9, and when Hitler was at his bunker, he would obsessively walk around it and inspect it. It seemed he might have despaired of the Germans, whom he blamed for their situation, because they were not strong enough, and so he neglected them.

Reports from SD agents on the public's mood at that time did show that the "Hitler Myth" was starting to fade.

Goebbels, who knew of Hitler's unstable state, then saw himself as the most important person in the Reich and the leader closest to the people, and he hoped that was how he would go down in the history books. While other leaders of the Nazi party started preparing alibis for themselves for the day after their defeat, Goebbels stuck to his guns and believed that that would make him a national hero.

During the last stage of the war, it seemed that German military policy was dictated not by military experts, but rather by politicians and ideologists. According to the German historian Wilhelm Deist, for Hitler's military commanders, the war remained a matter of battles, and tragically, their talent and tactical ability only helped prolong the apocalypse. At the beginning of 1945, there were efforts to send as many able men as possible to the front and to work in manufacturing ammunition. This move did not help win the war, but only prolonged the regime's life and the Germans' suffering.

This last year was characterized by governmental chaos, derived—among other things—from Hitler's life and work style: his unconventional nighttime work hours, his extensive absences from the nerve center of Berlin (Hitler spent most of his time at his "Wolf's Den," the Wolfschanze, in East Prussia), his intolerance and tendency towards drama and overreaction, his separation and lack of engagement with what was happening in the Reich, and his unstable and unpredictable behavior. All these things were projected onto the demeanor of the entire Nazi leadership and caused cracks in the regime.

An example of that came on July 20, 1944, when Hitler exposed his generals' opposition to the regime and its leader. Following the assassination attempt, Hitler's suspicion that betrayal within the army was everywhere grew into a deep belief. On the other hand, the failure of that conspiracy strengthened his belief that fate was on his side and that he was the right person to keep fulfilling a historic task, as he gave a speech before his officers about a month prior, on June 22, stressing that only those who were most fit would survive. He added that the Jews were "no more," that surrendering at this point would mean the annihilation of the Germans, and that "this new country will never surrender."

Hitler spoke once in the presence of Goebbels about the attempt on his life at Bürgerbräukeller, the large beer hall in Munich, in November 1939. Something irrational suddenly made him leave the place. He did not know why he had left, but everyone who stayed at the hall got hurt. Thirteen minutes stood between him and the death prepared for him by Georg Elser, a simple, 36-year-old, working-class German, who seemingly acted alone. And so, he was saved. Georg Elser, a construction worker and carpenter from Württemberg, feared a war was coming—he viewed it as inevitable under Nazi rule—and began thinking how it could be prevented in order to improve the state of workers in Germany. He realized he could make that happen only by taking out the Nazi leadership: Hitler, Goebbels, and Göring.

Elser decided to carry out the assassination and would start with the head tyrant himself. He hid a bomb in the hall where Hitler was supposed to give his traditional annual speech. On the day of November 8, 1939, Hitler did give a speech. He started speaking at 8:10 p.m. and finished at 9:07 p.m. He would usually stay and speak to the participants, but this time, unexpectedly, due to rough weather forecast, he left the room to make the 9:31 p.m. train back to Berlin. At 9:20 p.m. the bomb went off. Eight men were killed and 63 were injured. "The Führer was miraculously saved" was the headline of the *Völkischer Beobachter* on November 10. Hitler declared that he would not die until the historic task was complete, which was what fate had selected him for.

According to historian Joachim Fest, Hitler did not have a calculated plan for self-destruction, but it was rather "a chain reaction of hasty actions, outbursts of rage, and hysterical crying," followed by a string of commands, the first being the "Nero Decree," named after the Roman emperor. According to the tale, Nero watched over the Great Fire of Rome in 64 A.D. from his palace. The order was also called "Scorched Earth" (*Verbrannte Erde*). Hitler instituted it on March 19, 1945, and intended that it destroy all vital means of living in Germany: military facilities, transportation, communication, banks, industry, and food supplies. The logic behind it was to leave the enemy nothing but desert and wilderness, so that, when the war ended, so too would the German people. Hitler tied the fate of his people with his own, as he meant to take his entire nation down into his own doom.[255]

However, during the last year of the war, Hitler hoped to hold on and that a rift would open between the Western Allied forces and the Soviets, a rift that would bring about a global political shift and open up a new chapter in the campaign for World War II: a war between the Western Allied forces and Russia.[256] As Goebbels wrote in his diary: "Our task is to stay on our feet, no matter what. The crisis at the enemy camp has grown to significant proportions, but the question still remains: will it erupt while we can still defend ourselves? It is then, an assumption for a successful end to the war, that the rift at the enemy camp will indeed erupt before we fall down to the ground."[257]

Hitler saw the sudden death of U.S. President Franklin Delano Roosevelt on April 12, 1945, as further confirmation that fate was favoring Germany. Goebbels called Hitler the following day and congratulated him: "The stars have revealed to us that there will be a turn in our favor during the second half of April," he said. One of Hitler's acquaintances, Gerhard Herrgesell, who was himself at the bunker at the time, spoke of Hitler's reaction to the news: "How can I define it? One can only call it crazy. He was jumping back and forth in great joy saying 'Isn't that what I always said? I had a premonition.' I remember feeling awkward that a statesman would lose his restraint and jump around in such a childish manner."[258] Hitler brought up the miracle that had saved Frederick the Great in 1762, when Empress Yelisaveta suddenly died in the middle of the Seven Years' War, causing Prussia to gain military dominance in Europe.

A few days later, on April 20, Göring and Ribbentrop said farewell to Hitler and left Berlin. Two days later, Magda Goebbels arrived at the bunker with her six little children. Her relatives, as well as Hitler himself, tried to convince her to leave Berlin and save herself and her children, but she was unwilling to do so. Hitler held the last situation meeting at the bunker on April 22, 1945 and declared his intention to stay in Berlin and await the end. He acknowledged his situation's inevitability but was unwilling to take upon himself the initiative that would end the war. He wanted to lift the historical responsibility for the catastrophe off himself, which meant surrender. He was only able to postpone it, not avoid it.[259]

In the isolated world of the bunker in the besieged Berlin, Hitler held on to the unrealistic illusion that Goebbels's propaganda had created. It is possible that the news of Benito Mussolini's execution on April 29 drove him to the decision to commit suicide and make sure that his body would be burned, in order to prevent himself from falling into his enemies' hands. After being kicked and spat upon, the dead bodies of Mussolini, his mistress Clara Petacci and other Fascists were hung upside down in *Piazzale Loreto,* the major town square in Milan. Then the bodies were stoned by civilians. After receiving the news about the Italian leader, Goebbels told his deputy, Neumann: "This is the proof, should you need any, that you must not fall into their hands under any circumstances! If we were to lay our hands on Stalin or Churchill, the Führer would place them under honorable arrest in one of the forts. Aren't we, 'the barbarians,' better people after all?"[260]

Hitler committed suicide, along with his lover Eva Braun, on April 30, and per his orders their bodies were cremated. Before he died, Hitler appointed Goebbels Chancellor of Germany in his will, intending that he be the last in a line of Chancellors starting with Bismarck. Goebbels was Chancellor for only one day. He sent a letter to Admiral Karl Dönitz, in which he informed him of the Führer's death and his appointment as President of the Reich; this was his last political act.

That very night, after a conversation with Martin Bormann, Hans Krebs, Wilhelm Burgdorf, and Artur Axmann, Goebbels decided to start negotiating with Stalin on conditions to end the war. He wrote of Hitler's death and new appointments to Nazi leadership to the Soviet Secretary of State and called for a Russian-German cease fire and negotiations for the surrender of Germany. Stalin rejected the proposal and demanded that Germany surrender unconditionally.[261]

On one of the last days of his life, Goebbels told his deputy: "Remember my words, Neumann, what you witness today is a far greater historical drama that cannot be compared to any event in this century or any other, unless you go all the way back to Golgotha."[262] It seems that in saying so, Goebbels wanted to compare the last chapter of the lives of the Third Reich leaders to the Via Dolorosa Jesus endured on his way to the cross. Goebbels asked to be etched into history as the greatest symbol of loyalty to Hitler and the German people. He planned his death and that of his family in advance. He notified one of his deputies, Günther Schwägermann, that he and Magda were planning to commit suicide and asked that Schwägermann ensure their bodies be completely burned, so as to not fall into the hands of the Russians.

The day before Hitler's suicide, Magda consulted his personal physician, Dr. Ludwig Stumpfegger, and SS Deputy Chief Doctor, Dr. Helmut Gustav Kuntz. She asked to know how she could poison her six children quickly and painlessly. The following day, May 1, she laid the children in their beds, and with Dr. Stumpfegger present, she poisoned them with drops of hydrogen cyanide, with someone holding the children's mouths open. It appeared that the oldest daughter Helga tried to resist. "After the Führer and National-Socialism had gone, this world would no longer be worth living in, which is why I brought the children here," Magda wrote to her son, Harald, to explain her actions. "They are too good to live in the world that will follow, and the merciful God will understand me should I deliver them myself."

At around eight p.m., Goebbels put on his hat and his gloves, and went out of the bunker to the Chancellor Chamber's garden, along with his wife. She was wearing the golden Party badge Hitler had given her three days before. Just beforehand, he had told the radio operator, Rochus Misch, "*Les jeux sont faint,*" which means "the chips are down/ the bets have been made". He meant "the fate is out of my hands." The couple committed suicide by swallowing cyanide capsules, and an SS man shot them. A few soldiers spilled gasoline on their bodies and set them on fire. However, the Soviets, who arrived the following day, had no trouble identifying their burnt bodies and also found the bodies of their six children.

The following day, on May 2, the last Berlin Defense Area commander, Helmuth Weidling, reported from Berlin: "On April 30, the Führer ended his life by abandoning all who swore allegiance to him. According to the Führer's command, you German soldiers are willing to keep fighting for Berlin, even though you have run out of ammunition and the overall state shows that struggle is pointless. I order all resistance to stop immediately. Every further hour of fighting increases the terrible torment of Berlin's population and our injured soldiers. In agreement with the high command of the Soviet forces, I demand you stop fighting at once."[263]

Seven days later, Fieldmarshal Wilhelm Keitel, commander of the Wehrmacht High Command (OKW), signed the document of surrender: Germany surrendered unconditionally.

Despite the military defeats, the aerial bombings of Germany's cities and the disintegration of Nazi leadership during the last year of the war, at this period the extermination of the Jews in the face of doom was accelerated. For Example, with the invasion of Hungary on March 19, 1944, the biggest free Jewish population left in Europe fell into Germany's hands. The Nazis began an expedited operation to send Hungary's Jews to the Auschwitz-Birkenau extermination camp. Special railways were designated for that purpose, an abandoned gas chamber was restored and pits dug next to it, to burn the bodies in. Raul Hilberg shows that, in the twelve months from April 1943 to March 1944, about 160,000 Jews arrived in Auschwitz, and almost 585,000 in the few months between April 1944 and November of the same year. More Jews had been sent to Auschwitz in those eight months than in the two years before them.[264]

The gas chamberes and crematoriums at the camp worked to full capacity. In August 1944, 10,000 of Hungary's Jews were gassed in Auschwitz every day.[265] The killing continued until the camp was liberated by the Russians on January 27, 1945. When the deportations from Hungary ended, large transports still arrived from elsewhere. When Łódź Ghetto was liquidated in the summer of 1944, 60,000 of its occupants were sent to Auschwitz. The Chełmno extermination camp was reopened for that purpose. The Jews were transported in two main waves: on June 23, and on August 7. The destination was then changed, and the later transports were sent to Auschwitz.

The transports loaded with Jews came even from remote places, such as the Greek islands of Rhodes and Kos, whose 1,800 Jews were transported to Auschwitz in the summer of 1944. They were killed on the day of their arrival.[266] On April 17, 1945, The Gestapo was ordered to execute the sick prisoners in Abtnaudorf, one of Buchenwald's sub-camps, who were left when the camp was evacuated. SS Volkssturm forces gathered the prisoners into one of the baracks. They doused the building with gasoline and set it on fire. The prisoners struggled desperately to survive. Some managed to jump outside through the windows and get over the camp fence. Others died in a hail of bullets. The American soldiers who arrived shortly afterwards were presented with a horrific sight. The area was littered with burned or half-burned bodies and the corpses of those who had been shot. The number of victims remains unclear to this day. The bones of 84 men were later buried. At least 67 prisoners survived the massacre. These examples demonstrate that, even in the last days of the war, instruction were sent from the Reich Main Security Office to exterminate the remaining enemies of the Reich.[267]

Additionally, in the last months of the war, the Nazis took those of the camps' prisoners who managed to survive until then on death marches. On January 18, 1945, the remaining prisoners of Auschwitz were taken on such a march. Those who could not go on were shot on the spot. These marches happened in the span of four months, and many of the survivors remember them as the low points of the hell they went through. According to estimates, about a third of the 714,200 prisoners remaining in the camps in January 1945 perished in the marches.[268]

It is interesting to mention that, during that year, there was also significant acceleration in German bio-medical research. The Reich's Research Council even made it easier to transfer military researchers and doctors to civilian research facilities, in order to expedite current research. Many academics felt the last stages of the war would provide golden research opportunities and picked up the pace. When it got harder to find animals to be used for experiments, the temptation to use human subjects grew. In that last stage, German doctors used children in medical experiments, as a group that could not rise up and object to the exploitation.[269]

At the same time, the Germans continued the process of covering the traces of the mass murders. The operation was called "Aktion 1005"—a code name for an extensive operation that began in fall 1943. It was lead by SS commander Paul Blobel and was classified top secret. The prisoners who worked on the operation, the *Sonderkommandos*, were killed as soon as they finished their work. If policemen from the local Gendarmerie were present, they were killed as well. The closer the Allied armies advanced into Germany, the more extensive the operation became.[270]

The "heaven" the Nazis tried to create with the historical confrontation between the sons of the Aryan race—played out by the men of the SS—and the Jewish sub-race, took place in Auschwitz, where two opposing things were housed: an utopian plan and a hell on earth,[271] which reached its peak during the last year of the war in the face of impending defeat and doom.

Selection on the platform at Birkenau, Poland, May 27, 1944. Yad Vashem Photos Archive

Jews waiting in a grove near gas chamber no. 4 prior to their extermination, Birkenau, Poland, May 1944. Yad Vashem Photos Archive

CHAPTER FOUR

Final Triumph versus "Final Solution"

At the end of the nineteenth century and the beginning of the twentieth, German thinkers warned that Germany was on the brink of a change that would affect all areas of life—society, politics, culture, and the economy. So, it was from the depths of the doom of German defeat in World War I, 1918 that a strong German Reich was expected to reemerge. Möller van den Bruck (1876–1925) suggested it be named *The Third Reich*. That was the name of his book (*Das Dritte Reich*), published in 1922, in which he attacked Liberalism, Social-Democrats, and the daily corruption of political powers in Germany. He called for a revolution that would change the situation.[272] The biblical scholar Paul de Lagarde also looked to strengthen the German people by creating a unity that was both political and spiritual. In his collection of essays, *German Writings*, he offered to achieve this unity by maintaining what was considered the existence of the German people and the nation's life force—their blood. He saw the nation as a spiritual essence, an ideal that bound people together and should be fought for. According to him it was in war, with its limitless call for blood, that the people received their strength and vitality.

Another philosopher, Julius Langbehn (1851–1907), reprimanded intellectualism, science, and modern culture in his book *Rembrandt as Teacher*,[273] and called for a return to the essence of the creating German people, to revive the German past through artistic creation, which he regarded as the supreme good. Langbehn saw Rembrandt as the personification of the cultural ideal. To him, Rembrandt symbolized an ideal that would be appropriate for a perfect German, the unparalleled artist, and an antithesis to modern culture, a prophet of the new society he hoped would be established, based on art, ingenuity, and power. The superior qualities of the German *volk* were naturally given, they coursed through the blood and were passed on from father to son. Art could burst out of the strong German people and the organic community it created. In the decadent atmosphere of the turn of the century, Langbehn became an obsessive anti-Semite. He described the Jews as the total opposite of the "creative" Germans.[274] According to him, the atrophy of Germany came from the modern lifestyle, which destroyed the traditional culture, and which was the immediate responsibility of the Jews.[275]

German sociologist and philosopher Eugen Dühring (1833–1921) also blamed the Jews for the Germans' poor condition. In his book *The Jewish Question as a Racial, Moral, and cultural Question*,[276] he wrote of artistic and moral atrophy rooted in every Jewish individual. Dühring's unique contribution to the anti-Semitic discussion was in turning the cultural dimension into a racial category, emphasizing that there was "no way back," since a line of war was already woven between the forces of Jewish materialism and the Germans who acted according to an ancient *volkian* instinct that would bring about social solidarity once the Jews were removed.[277]

The harsh trauma of the humiliating defeat the Germans experienced at the end of World War I had to have a reasonable explanation; the downfall had to have meaning. One of the people who tried to provide an explanation was the German General Erich Ludendorff (1865–1937), a member of Hitler's inner circle. He wrote that during World War I, the Jews took advantage of the window of opportunity and took over the German economy: "They acquired a dominant influence in the 'war corporations'...which gave them the occasion to enrich themselves at the expense of the German people and to take possession of the German economy, in order to achieve one of the power goals of the Jewish people".[278]

Ludendorff developed a "Total War" theory in which he claimed that "War is the highest expression of the racial will to live," and that the leader of a total war had the right to claim the unity of the people as "the duty of the country to a total policy." He would do so by oppressing any resistance and closing the country's borders. According to him, propaganda was an important tool in total war, inflaming the general population to fight for the country and strengthen morale.[279]

During that period of time, anti-Semitism also spread in academia, among other reasons due to the influence of Heinrich von Treitschke's creed, according to which the Jews—who were unable to establish a country of their own—were assimilated into Germany and thus weakened it from within. He called on Germans to be proud of their special national qualities and fend off the grotesquerie of Judaism.[280]

At the turn of the twentieth century, traditional anti-Semitic ideology received reinforcement on the anthropological level as well, for instance through the works of anthropologist and theoretician Georges Vacher de Lapouge (1854–1936), who developed social anthropology (*Sozialanthropologie*). He turned the racist anti-Semitic theory into a "scientific" one, and claimed that, in the current age, Europe was in its greatest religious and moral crisis since the beginning of mankind, all the way to suicidal nihilism and utter pessimism.[281]

Similarly, the dialogue between Dietrich Eckart and Hitler, *The Bolshevism from Moses to Lenin: A Dialogue between Hitler and Myself* (*Der Bolschewismus von Moses bis Lenin: Zwiegespräch zwischen Adolf Hitler und Mir*), was published in 1924 and presented Hitler's opinions on the Jews. The apocalyptic dimension attributed to Judaism was the key issue of the dialogue. Hitler saw the Jew as an evil force acting throughout history. According to him:

> One can only understand the Jew when one knows what his ultimate goal is. And that goal is, beyond world domination, the annihilation of the world. He must wear down all the rest of mankind, he persuades himself, in order to prepare a paradise on earth. He has made himself believe that only he is capable of this great task, and,

> considering his ideas of paradise, that is certainly so. But one sees, if only in the means which he employs, that he is secretly driven to something else. While he pretends to himself to be elevating mankind, he torments men to despair, to madness, to ruin. If a halt is not ordered, he will destroy all men. His nature compels him to that goal, even though he dimly realizes that he must thereby destroy himself. There is no other way for him; he must act thus. This realization of the unconditional dependence of his own existence upon that of his victims appears to me to be the main cause for his hatred. To be obliged to try and annihilate us with all his might, but at the same time to suspect that that must lead inevitably to his own ruin—therein lies, if you will, the tragedy of Lucifer.[282]

However, the doom and descent could be prevented, "redeeming" Germany and even all of

Europe from this Jewish danger. The "redemptive anti-Semitism," according to Saul Friedländer's explanation, came from the fear of racial atrophy, meaning the entrance of Jews into politics, society, and German blood. The religious belief in redemption meant a fight to life and death against the Jews. The redemption of the Germans would come once they were released from the burden of the Jews. Friedländer claims the source of that new movement of apocalyptic anti-Semitism comes from the convergence of Germanic Christianity, neo-romanticism, the mystical worship of sacred Aryan blood, and extremely conservative nationalism—at the Bayreuth Circle. Hitler turned Bayreuth into the pilgrimage site of German culture.[283]

In this context, *redemption* became a leitmotif in the ideology of composer Richard Wagner, and the disappearance of the Jews was the key component of his vision. The Jew was, according to him, a symbol of earthly temptations and had left its humanity behind. Wagner's student, Houston Stewart Chamberlain, developed his master's ideas after Wagner's death.

He called for a birth of a German Christian religion, purified from the Jewish spirit within it, and even claimed that Jesus himself was not Jewish, but rather, an Aryan. His assumption was that the salvation of Aryan Christianity would be accomplished only by eradicating the Jews. He wrote:

> No arguing about 'humanity' can alter the fact that this means a struggle.
>
> Where the struggle is not waged with cannon-balls, it goes on silently in the heart of society... But this struggle, silent though it be, is above all others a struggle for life and death.[284]

Richard Wagner himself was influenced by two main sources: Charles Darwin's ideas on the survival of the fittest, which were spread throughout Germany by zoologist and philosopher Ernst Häckel, and the racist thinking of Joseph Arthur de Gobineau (1816–1882). In his book, *An Essay on the Inequality of the*

Human Races,[285] Gobineau claimed that a tragic and irreversible historical process of mixing superior and inferior races necessarily led to the decline of the former. Within his racially pessimistic creed, he constructed a new interpretation of global history, claiming that interracial blending was the root of decline and death.[286] The Jew (*der Jude*) was presented in Nazi ideology not only as dangerous in spirit, but as contaminated, dangerous, and dirty, so much so that it caused actual physical repulsion.[287] The perception of the German Aryan body necessarily required removing the other body—the Jew, who was considered a killing factor, threatening the eternity of the living German body.[288]

An example of that can be seen in Wagner's anti-Semitic essay, 'Judaism in Music" (*Das Judenthum in der Musik*), published in 1851, in which the author wanted to "clarify to ourselves what that unnoticeable, repulsive element is, which we feel in the Jew's personality and essence. That justifies the instinctive repulsion, which is utterly strong and decisive."[289] In an addition to this essay, called "Clarifying 'Judaism in Music,'" Wagner claimed they should prevent "the atrophy of our culture by expelling the element that causes decay through violent means."[290]

In the closing sentence of "Judaism in Music," Wagner calls to the Jews: "Lend an unreserved hand to this blood struggle while losing yourselves—then we will be united, and nothing will come between us, but notice: there is only one possible redemption from the curse you carry, the redemption of Ahasuerus—doom!"[291]

Wagner used here the word *Der Untergang*, which could also be translated as downfall or annihilation, thus offering a solution that could be widely interpreted as the Jews' desired fate: spiritual or physical doom. Wagner was the prophet of German culture in his time and a supreme ideological authority. He wanted to go back to the ideal Germanic past, which was ruined by the greedy culture and loss of values, led by the Jews.

This German anti-Semitic racist tradition was present with the rise of Nazi Germany. We must try to understand whether the sense of doom that spread through the Nazi leadership in the last year of the war—a sense similar to that at the turn of the century—influenced what went on in the extermination camps and the Germans' sense of urgency to end this "endeavor" of the extermination of the Jews. Could we find some sort of "logic" behind the acceleration of the methodical extermination of the Jews at that time, during a period of downfall and doom at the last year of the war?

A possible answer to this, as mentioned, lies in examining Goebbels's propaganda machine, which provided the legitimacy to continue fighting at the front and exterminating the Jews despite the defeats. According to this propaganda machine, the start of the war and the extermination of the Jews were intertwined. Germany could defeat Communism—the destruction of which resembled that of the Jews—through war and could also activate the final solution for the problem that had gnawed at Germany's very core: the Jews. Hitler was smart to realize that fulfilling his grand obsessive plan of total elimination, a methodical genocide of the Jews, would have to be set on the right ground. Anti-Semitic propaganda actions began long before his rise to power, and as a global war erupted, theory became practice. In war, there will be victims, and as far as the Germans were concerned, their goal was to defeat and kill the enemy, and they did not have to answer for that.

In doing this, Nazism sought to ameliorate the trauma of Germany's defeat in World War I, which was followed by many years of recovery. One of the key claims was that the Jews were to be blamed for that defeat. Therefore, on the brink of defeat during the second "Great War," the relationship between anti-Semitism and the "redemption by doom" motive was enhanced. Hitler considered the mistakes that had led to the humiliating defeat of the Imperial Reich in the "Great War" already in his book, *Mein Kampf.* The mass killing during the war influenced the catastrophic-apocalyptic mindset of Europe back then. Among the reasons that brought about collapse and moral atrophy, Hitler emphasized the question of race as he wrote:

> The ultimate and most profound reason for the German downfall is to be found in the fact that the racial problem was ignored and that its importance in the historical development of nations was not grasped. For the events that take place in the life of nations are not due to chance, but are the natural results of the effort to conserve and multiply the species and the race, even though men may not be able consciously to picture in their minds the profound motives of their conduct.[292]

The "superior" Germans should have guarded themselves from intermixing with other "inferior" races and maintained the purity of their blood. In this nihilism-soaked atmosphere of spiritual and artistic descent, and sense of atrophy and pessimism, anti-Semitism was used as a possible explanation. Thus a "removal" of Jews from the lives of Germans was seen as the desired solution.

War was part of a sophisticated camouflage to perform the great extermination. Even at the height of extermination, when the bridges were indeed burnt behind the Germans as Goebbels declared,[293] Nazi leadership continued to insist on fighting the war on one hand and operating the extermination mechanism on the other. Bernd Wegner suggests that Hitler linked military triumphs with the "Final Solution"—he believed he could accomplish it only if he won the war. Following Germany's military deterioration, especially after the defeat at Stalingrad, victory was no longer foremost in Hitler's concerns, but rather the mission of keeping the Allied Forces away from the extermination camps, so the Germans could finish what they had started. On the one hand, the war was maintained to protect the existence of the camps, and, on the other hand, the camps were the psychological border that kept the Germans from starting negotiations: if the Nazi regime were to negotiate and its deeds became publicly known, there would be a cost. It was under this assumption that they asked to expedite the rate of extermination at the end of the war.[294] As Goebbels wrote: "As I impressed urgently on the Führer, if we can really no longer hold out in the West, then our last political war plan collapses, for if the Anglo-Americans reach central Germany, they would not have even the smallest reason to enter into talks with us."[295]

Opening the gates of the extermination camps and bringing new Jewish groups into the circle of extermination, such as the transport of Hungarian Jewry to Auschwitz-Birkenau, was a lot of work for the Germans and required significant resources, which were "justified" if the reasons were ideological rather than just practical: European Jewry had to be exterminated to the very last, since Germany's situation would improve by transporting the remaining Jews for extermination. Distanced from their military defeats and the bombardments on the German home front, the mechanism of extermination remained efficient and fully functioning. Hitler acted according to plans that were mostly unattainable dreams, such as conquering the USSR or rebuilding the city of Linz. Cleansing Europe of Jews was perhaps one of his more attainable goals, perhaps even the most effective plan he came up with, and a plan he would continue for as long as possible. He even ordered it to be continued in his political testament, which he wrote on April 29, 1945, less than 24 hours before he committed suicide:

> But before everything else, I call upon the leadership of the nation and those who follow it to observe the racial laws most carefully, to fight mercilessly against the poisoners of all the people of the world, International Jewry.

Despite his intense hatred of the Jews as shown at the end of his days, the circumstances of the decision to start the "Final Solution" are still in dispute. Mommsen claims that the Holocaust was not the result of an established plan, but rather evolved in stages for a long time and escalated until it developed an internal dynamic of its own. He believes Nazi ideology, anti-Semitic propaganda, and authoritative elements were not enough to explain how it happened. According to him, such genocide could have also happened under different social conditions.[296]

But perhaps this argument is more complicated than might seem when examining occurrences in the last year of the Third Reich, during which the Nazi leadership dealt with frightened bombarded civilians as well as a Führer who was losing his mind—yet still held onto the policy of extermination. One of the main reasons for this leadership's strength was the place propaganda held and the performance of the Minister of Propaganda, Goebbels himself, who caused the continuation of the Holocaust, and urged the Germans to continue the extermination of the Jews even after experiencing harsh defeats, and even after realizing that victory was impossible.

Anti-Semitic tradition—which was rooted deeply into Nazi ideology—created something new in the time of Hitler's rule, a form of hatred for the Jews that justified genocide. It was possible that "something new" wasn't simply created in 1930s–1940s Germany, but rather that the time and place and people in power brought on that "civilizational fracture." It was not the hatred for the Jews that changed, but the objective conditions for transforming it from mere theory into actual practice. A key and even crucial role in these objective conditions was played by Nazi propaganda, as a tool that, on one hand, made extermination legitimate and an act of consensus, while on the other hand, it created a "new morality"—a murderous morality. As the German-born Jewish political philosopher Hannah Arendt described the frenzy of killing, in her book on the Adolf Eichmann's trial:

> What Eichmann referred to as the "whirl of death" that lay on Germany after the massive losses at Stalingrad— the saturation bombing of German cities... certainly contributed to the numbing, or to be more precise, the elimination of conscience, if there were any of it left while all that was happening."[297]

The importance and influence of Joseph Goebbels on the course of events and the decision-making was somewhat set aside in the Third

Reich's general historiography. Compared with other prominent figures, such as Göring, Himmler, Rosenberg, and Speer, it seems Goebbels influenced the course of things during the last part of the war no less than they. He wished to be written down and remembered in history, and when given the chance, he put his all into developing a sophisticated propaganda machine that carried great weight in developing the face of the Third Reich. Goebbels had a key role in creating the "Führer Myth"; he was the one who preached to eliminate the "Judeo-Bolshevik" monster from the very beginning of the war; he was the one who enlightened the Germans about the wide range of dangers that would befall them if they did not eliminate this monster. Finally, in the German people's darkest hour, it was Goebbels who gathered all his might and abilities to provide the suffering people with a sense of meaning to their defeat and doom, hoping history would also view it that way and that he would be remembered thus as a kind of hero, supporting, and comforting his nation.

Goebbels was part of the "Total War" leadership as of July 1944, after the miraculous saving of Hitler from the attempt on his life. He contributed to it with the propaganda he developed and spread, a war against Judaism and the Bolshevik forces behind which it stood, and which the entire people had to take part in. The "Final Solution" was planned in such a way that would involve the entire German people in this huge crime against humanity, bind them to their leadership, and make them fight to the death. Despite addressing masses of Germans, Goebbels himself became enslaved to his own propaganda, which ultimately backfired on him. His struggle to convince Hitler to further act for totalization and radicalization of the war, his repetitive attempts to get rid of figures he did not like, such as Göring and Ribbentrop, and most of all during the final stage of the war, his planning the production of the last scene of his own life—the collective suicide of him and his family—were born of a will to leave a mark of loyalty and bravery on history, to be a symbol and example of loyalty to the Führer and to Germany.

EPILOGUE

To understand the essence of the paradox which marks the last year of World War II, in which Germany faced the final defeat with the full awareness of its doom, while the extermination of the Jews continued and was even accelerated, one must return to the historical discussion of just when the decision for the "Final Solution" was made. The answer to that question will help to answer the following questions: was the war an excuse for a planned extermination of the Jews, or was it only once the war was in progress that the Germans acknowledged the opportunity and decided on the "Final Solution"? Did the extermination begin based on the fine victories of the Wehrmacht, while Hitler was intoxicated with victory and confident in achieving his goals, or was it those military defeats that inspired it all? If the latter, was the actual goal of the extermination a form of encouragement for Germany in its hour of defeat?

Germany's situation began deteriorating once the Sixth Army was defeated at Stalingrad and its painful downfall began. It suffered additional military defeats and bombardment of its cities and citizens during the last year of the war. Germany's material and mental states reached new lows in the last year of the war. The German army suffered heavy losses in the summer of 1944: Between June and October, 1,082,197 soldiers fell in battle (an average of 7,200 soldiers every day); around 1.4 million German soldiers fell in battles between January 1945 and the end of the war in May. (Around 450,000 soldiers died in January 1945 alone. More than 370,000 lost their lives in the last five weeks of the war).[298]

The defeat at Stalingrad was the military and psychological low point of the war, after which the "Hitler Myth" began to dissolve. However, the SD reports showed that, even during the fighting, only a third of the German population was willing to admit that the war was lost. The rest of the Germans did not even imagine giving up on the fight until the very end. For them, Hitler remained a symbol of hope and resilience.

Some believe the sources of any rational approach to the systematic extermination of the Jews during the Holocaust should be looked for in Hitler's war plans, which changed after the swift victory of Germany over France in the summer of 1940. This victory, which resulted in Hitler's inauguration as "Supreme Commander" and "The Architect of Victory" with his Blitzkrieg strategy, is the key to understanding his ultimate goals. Victory increased the faith of the Nazi leadership in the Wehrmacht, presented as an invincible army, and this faith influenced the decision to continue the war and reaching for the next objective—conquering the USSR. Hitler himself was responsible for the military planning and demanded a quick and brutal solution to the problem of Germany's *Lebensraum*, "living space," that would establish it as the greatest European power.

Conquering the East was meant to maintain the "racial value" of the German people, among other things, and it remained an important target for Hitler. The first of twenty-five sections of the Nazi party's platform demanded "unifying all Germans into one Germany, based on the people's right to self-definition."[299] However, after the United States entered the war, turning it from a European war into a World War, the tables turned: instead of waiting for the end of the war to deal with the "Jewish problem," the Nazi regime decided to address it immediately, fulfilling Hitler's prophecy in his speech of January 30, 1939 that if another World War were to break out, its consequence would mean the extermination of the Jews. Goebbels also placed the blame for starting the war on the Jews, in an article from November 1941: "The Jews wanted their war and now they got it... global Jewry was mistaken when adding the powers at its disposal to the war, and is now gradually experiencing a process of extermination, which they would have carried out upon us without thinking twice, had they only the power to do so."[300]

And so, instead of a "Final Solution" via final victory, it was now the other way around: Germany would win the war only once the "Final Solution" of exterminating the Jews was achieved. According to historian Christian Gerlach, this was also the reason the Wannsee Conference was postponed a month, from December 16, 1941, to January 20, 1942, since they had to reorganize following the "Final Solution" decision. Hans Frank, Governor of the General government, said in a meeting in Krakow on December 16, 1941—about two weeks after the U.S. forces entered the war: "As for the Jews, I basically expect them to disappear. They have to be gone... what will be the fate of the Jews? You think they will be settled in development villages in Ostland? They told us in Berlin, why do you need this trouble; neither Ostland nor Reichskommissariat would have them, eliminate them yourselves."[301]

According to this approach, the extermination of the Jews began in an improvised manner and was not the outcome of long-term planning or a secret order. Erich Goldhagen also believes that the Holocaust did not take place due to a blind hatred of the Jewish people, but by a logical Machiavellian approach. He claims that Nazi anti-Semitism was a combination of rational calculations and an irrational fanaticism. The German historian Götz Aly adds that the "Führer's order" was unnecessary as the "Final Solution," even if there was one, was ineffective. The decision was made on a wider process, in which the senior and minor officials of the relevant institutes of the Third Reich took part. According to Aly's version, when the occupations began, the Germans uprooted many local populations—among them Jews—in order to settle German citizens in their stead, "Volksdeutsche." Only in the next stage, when they realized there was no way to accommodate all the uprooted people, did they begin thinking of a more effective solution. That was how the mass killings started, a method that had been implemented even earlier against unwanted German populations in Operation T4 (the euthanasia of sick and disabled Germans). The official order for Operation T4 execution, signed by Hitler, was given on the day the war broke out, September 1, 1939.[302] The Russian campaign provided the Nazis with additional practical experience in eliminating unwanted populations, such as the extermination of Soviet prisoners of war and of the "suspect population" in the East. From that point, the road to the systematic extermination of Jews was merely logical. Hans Mommsen also believed so, claiming that the "Commissar Order" Hitler issued on June 6, 1941—in which he ordered the deaths of all Soviet POW officers—and the beginning of the Einsatzgruppen's actions to eliminate Jews they encountered in the USSR marked the beginning of a new chapter.[303]

The 1922 book *Allowing the Destruction of Life Unworthy of Living*,[304] which heavily influenced the euthanasia operation, provided ideological justification for the murders. One of its authors, psychiatrist Alfred Hoche, claimed that, if the strong and talented sacrificed their lives for the nation in World War I, the sick and "inferior" must also make a similar sacrifice. This way, the negative selection, caused by the war, in which the "worthy" elements were killed, would be eliminated. He himself lost his only son to the war and used that tragic case to strengthen his claim.[305] The Germans defined the

Jews as a group "unworthy of living," and therefor paved the way for their extermination.

The terrible enigma of Adolf Hitler still has not been solved. This book attempts to examine the image of one of the people closest to him, Minister of Propaganda Joseph Goebbels, who remained loyal to Hitler and his way since they first joined forces in the 1920s and until the death of both. Goebbels was the pillar of Germany in its final hour. Then he committed suicide with his wife and children at the Berlin bunker. He believed that he would keep playing the role of his lifetime as a central figure in the history to be written.

Goebbels saw himself not only as an avid supporter of Hitler, but also as having influence on him and being the person who comforted him in his hour of need—in the last year of the war—as Hitler sank into madness and depression. So, he wrote in his diary: "I am telling the Führer all sorts of things about the aerial combat in Berlin, including nice anecdotes that make him very happy."[306]

Albert Speer, Minister of Armaments, also saw it this way: "Goebbels knows how to support Hitler, with great speaking abilities, polished sentences with perfectly placed ironies, excitement where Hitler expects there to be, sentimentality when obligated, with gossip and love affairs. He masterfully mixes it all up: theater, cinema, and ancient history. Hitler also allows him to speak about the Goebbels children... in detail."[307]

Goebbels was influenced by German historian and philosopher Oswald Spengler (1880–1936), who presented civilization as a circle of birth, maturity, and downfall that ends in death in his book *The Decline of the West* (1918–1922): "A person must acknowledge and face his unchanged fate with dignity and bravery. Stick it out to the end, remain in abandoned posts without hope or redemption, this is our duty... this is greatness... *a glorified end is the only thing no one can take from a person.*[308]

Indeed, the examination of the deteriorating Nazi leadership in the last year of the war in light of the military defeats and the severe damage to the German Homefront, attests to the irrational decision to keep holding on, sticking to goals until the very end, against all odds. This was manifested in the extermination of the Jews, among other things. Facing doom, the Nazi regime could pride itself on its "last success": exterminating additional hundreds of thousands of Jews. The regime prevented any chance of negotiating political terms to end the war and surrender, sacrificing the citizens of Germany and its soldiers on the shrine of Teutonic redemption to the sounds of Siegfried's funeral march in the last part of Richard Wagner's *Ring of the Nibelung*, *"The Twilight of the Gods"*, Götterdämmerung.

When an opportunity to negotiate with the Soviets was possible in March 1945, Goebbels clarified in his diary: "In principle we need not be averse to making use of such an opportunity. Nevertheless, the present moment is as bad a choice as it could be. I think, however, that it would be as well at least to talk to the Soviet Union's representative. But the Führer does not wish to. The Führer thinks that, for the present, it would be a sign of weakness if we were to meet the enemy's wishes on this point."[309]

Goebbels's propaganda lost its grip on reality in its last year. For instance, he said in one of his many speeches at the beginning of October 1944: "I know the events in the West have shocked the German people. It is completely understandable, since we have imagined military developments to be different than reality. Despite that, we are now not much worse than we were in September 1939, when this battle began."[310]

Goebbels used historical images to strengthen the German people and encourage them to hang on: "Hannibal once stood before the gates of Rome, without Rome surrendering... the plow of Rome went over what was once Carthage."[311] The message he was looking to convey was that, if Germany held on, it would eventually win.

When all chances of a final German victory were lost, Goebbels chose to tie his fate and that of his family with Hitler's, and planned their joint death. He sought to preserve the "Führer Myth" and give an air of ultimate self sacrifice to the supreme leader, as well as to his own image—to be the most wonderful example of German loyalty. If Goebbels hoped, through his diaries, to be the main historian of the Third Reich, indeed he wished to make his mark on its most glorious chapter, the "Twilight of the Gods": self-sacrifice against the background of Berlin, the burning down of Walhalla.

Once all hope of saving Germany was lost, Goebbels found meaning in the events of the last year of the war, in the sense of salvation achieved by the self-destruction of the German people, the "Thousand-Year Reich," which had come to an end only twelve years after its institution. Even though Germany was defeated in war, Goebbels's experiment had worked: millions of Germans followed an idea and ideology that eventually led to their ruin, continuing to support a leader whose physical and mental state deteriorated, though his charisma remained untouched, and they paid a heavy price for that.

According to Joachim Fest, Goebbels's career can be explained only through a deeply rooted contempt for humanity: "The cold, calculated, and cruel man at the top of the Nazi leadership was completely void of 'the burden of conscience.'" Goebbels was an opportunist who eventually became Hitler's greatest disciple.[312] Did he think the final chapter of the Nazi saga, which he helped lead and orchestrate, would help restore his and his Führer's honor and provide them with mystical auras? Would they be rewarded for jointly committing suicide, rewarded with eternal life by being written into history and being remembered as lofted gods?

Sebastian Haffner wrote sometime after the war: "The Berlin of 1945 was not the Carthage of 146 BC. It was a living city that went through purgatory on its way to one of its best times, and Goebbels's suicide seemed unfortunately irrelevant against that backdrop."[313]

The "Twilight of the Gods" that Goebbels created, into which he drew his wife and children, is not remembered in history as a great sacrifice of the most loyal genius. Goebbels created the "Führer Myth" and transformed Hitler into a person selected by providence to lead the German people. However, in the last year of the war, neither Hitler nor Goebbels seemed like gods, and their leadership skills were also in doubt. It seems that Goebbels realized that, and so decided to give them both a divine aura in death.

He did not see himself being captured by an enemy and brought to justice as another wicked dictator, sitting next to Göring, Hess, and Speer, waiting to be hanged in public with calls of contempt accompanying his last moments. However, despite the last staged scene at the bunker, its actors—Hitler and Goebbels—are remembered as dark spots on the history of the greatest tragedy that has ever plagued mankind. This scene, of the Goebbels couple's charred bodies and the bodies of their six children, was not taken from some heroic Wagnerian opera, but was nothing more than the Nazi master of illusion Joseph Goebbels's last, unsuccessful propaganda trick.

TIMELINE OF THE LIFE OF JOSEPH GOEBBELS

Germany, Party rally, Goebbels saluting in uniform.
Yad Vashem Photos Archive

October 29, 1897	Paul Joseph is born to Fritz and Maria Katerina in Rheydt, North Rhine-Westphalia.
1917–1921	Studies at the Bonn, Würzburg, Freiburg, and Heidelberg universities.

1921	Finishes his doctoral thesis on playwright Wilhelm von Schütz.
End of 1924	Joins the Nazi party.
October 26, 1926	Is appointed Gauleiter of Berlin.
1927	Becomes Editor-in-Chief of the "Der Angriff" newspaper.
April 28, 1928	Is appointed Head of Propaganda throughout Germany.
1929	Publishes his book, *Michael.*
February 23, 1930	Death of SS man Horst Wessel, whom Goebbels transforms into a martyr of the Nazi party.

December 19, 1931	Joseph Goebbels and Magda Quandt marry. Hitler is his best man.
September 1932	Goebbels's eldest daughter, Helga, is born; first of six children.
January 30, 1933	Nazi party seizes power; Hitler appointed Reich Chancellor.
March 13, 1933	Goebbels is appointed Minister of Propaganda and Public Enlightenment.
May 10, 1933	The great book burning in the plaza of the Berlin Opera House, orchestrated by Goebbels. "*The German people will have a new education from now on,*" he

	says in the speech he gives that evening.
1934	Publishes his books, *From the Kaiserhof to the Reich Chancellery* and *The Battle for Berlin*.
1936–1938	Has an affair with Czech actress Lída Baarová.
November 9, 1938	The Kristallnacht riots, encouraged by Goebbels.
November 1940	Goes to Prague and seeks to "make it a German city."
1941	Publishes his book *Die Zeit ohne Beispiel*, articles and speeches from 1939–1941.
November 16, 1941	His article "The Jews are Guilty" is published in the *Das Reich* newspaper. "The

	Jews are receiving a penalty that is certainly hard, but better than deserved," it states.
May 24, 1942	Goebbels claims that war in the East is unlike any other war before it. It is about triumph or doom (*Triumph oder Untergang*).
February 2, 1943	The Battle of Stalingrad ends in German defeat. About 150 thousand German soldiers are killed and another 113 thousand captured, from which only a few thousands ever return to Germany.
February 18, 1943	After Germany's defeat at Stalingrad, Goebbels speaks at the Berlin Sportpalast calling for Total War: "Rise

	up, and let the storm break loose!"
May 9, 1943	Publishes his article "The War and the Jews" in the *Das Reich* newspaper.
July 20, 1944	Operation Valkyrie, the failed assassination attempt on Hitler's life.
July 25, 1944	Hitler appoints Goebbels to the new position: *Reich Plenipotentiary for Total War.*
January 21, 1945	Publishes his article "Creators of the World's Misfortunes" in the *Das Reich* newspaper.
March 9, 1945	Goes to Görlitz to speak to soldiers, so they will continue to fight and stand their ground.

April 17, 1945	Screening of the movie *Kolberg*, Goebbels' last great creation.
April 21, 1945	Goebbels's last radio broadcast.
April 29, 1945	Hitler dictates his last will and testament, appointing Goebbels Chancellor of Germany before his suicide.
April 30, 1945	Hitler commits suicide with his newly-wedded wife, Eva Braun.
May 1, 1945	Goebbels and his wife Magda commit suicide in Berlin after poisoning their six children in Hitler's bunker.

NOTES

1 H. R. Trevor-Roper, *The New York Times,* March 14, 1948.

2 Sections of Goebbels's diary have been published in books such as (in publication order): Louis P. Lochner, *The Goebbels Diaries* (New York, 1948); Helmut Heiber, *Das Tagebuch von Joseph Goebbels 1925/26* (Stuttgart, 1960); Rolf Hochhuth (Hrsg.), *Joseph Goebbels: Tagebücher 1945: Die Letzten Aufzeichnungen* (Hamburg, 1977); Elke Fröhlich (Hrsg.), *Die Tagebücher von Joseph Goebbels* [hereafter: TBJG] (München, 1987–1996).

3 Michael Kater, "Inside Nazis: The Goebbels Diaries 1924–1941," *Canadian Journal of History* 25 (1990), 243.

4 Albert Speer, *Inside the Third Reich: Memories* (New York, 1970). Speer (1905–1981) was an architect by profession. In 1942 Hitler appointed him Minister of Armaments. In the Nuremberg trials at the end of the war, he was sentenced to twenty years' imprisonment. He was released in 1966, and about three years later he published his memoirs, which he had written in prison.

5 Joseph Goebbels, *Michael: Ein Deutsches Schicksal in Tagebuchblättern (München, Zentralverlag der NSDAP, 1929); Vom Kaiserhof zur Reichskanzlei: Eine historische Darstellung in Tagebuchblättern* (München, Zentralverlag der NSDAP, 1934).

6 Goebbels, *Vom Kaiserhof zur Reichskanzlei,* 308.

7 Viktor Reimann, *The Man who Created Hitler: Joseph Goebbels* (London, 1977), 3–4.

8 Wolfgang Goetz (1885–1955), *Neidhardt von Gneisenau* (1925).

9 *TBJG*, April 3, 1945.

10 Bernd Wegner (Hrsg.), *Wie Kriege Enden: Wege zum Frieden von der Antike bis zur Gegenwart* (Paderborn, 2002), xi.

11 Jay Baird, *To Die for Germany: Heroes in the Nazi Pantheon* (Indianapolis, 1990), 207–208. In World War I, Europe had to face an unprecedented number of casualties: approximately thirteen million people. For more on the battle casualties of this war and the attitude towards them that were developing in Europe, see George Mosse, *Fallen Soldiers: Reshaping the Memory of the World Wars* (New York, 1990).

12 There is some dispute regarding the year of publication, with one claim that it appeared in 1873.

13 Fritz Stern, *The Politics of Cultural Despair: A Study in the Rise of the Germanic Ideology* (Garden City, 1965), 76.

14 Ibid, 66.

15 Christopher Browning, *The Origins of the Final Solution: The Evolution of Nazi Jewish Policy, September 1939–March 1942* (Lincoln and Jerusalem, 2004), 309–314.

16 Christopher Browning, "The Political and Military Context of the Decisions regarding the 'Final

Solution,' 1939–1941." *Dapim for the Research of the Holocaust Period,* Vol. 8 (1990), 34.

17 Christian Gerlach, "The Wannsee Conference, the Fate of German Jews, and Hitler's Decision in Principle to Exterminate All European Jews," *The Journal of Modern History* 70 (4) (1998), 784. Gerlach bases his claim on an account of a meeting held between Hitler and Alfred Rosenberg on December 14, 1941, in which the two discussed changing a speech Rosenberg had prepared prior to the Japanese attack, and which had to be adjusted "now after the decision." Ibid, 783.

18 *TBJG*, December 13, 1941.

19 Tobias Jersak, "A Matter of Foreign Policy: 'Final Solution' and 'Final Victory' in Nazi Germany," *German History* 21 (3) (2003), 377–379.

20 *TBJG*, August 19, 1941.

21 Jersak, "A Matter of Foreign Policy," 381–382.

22 Ian Kershaw, *Hitler 1936–1945: Nemesis* (New York, 2000), 490–492.

23 Martin Broszat, "Hitler and the Genesis of the 'Final Solution': An Assessment of David Irving's Theses." *Yad Vashem Studies* 13 (1980), 75.

24 Sebastian Heffner, *The Meaning of Hitler* (New York, 1979).

25 Leni Yahil, *The Holocaust: The Fate of European Jewry, 1932–1945* (New York, 1990), 527.

26 Manfred Kehrig, "Die 6. Armee im Kessel von Stalingrad," in Jürgen Förster (Hrsg.), *Stalingrad: Ereignis-Wirkung-Symbol* (München, 1992), 109.

27 Jay Baird, *The Mythical World of Nazi Propaganda, 1939–1945* (Minneapolis, 1974), 184. For example, read the front page of the *Völkischer Beobachter* on February 4, 1943: "They died so Germany might continue to live."

28 Marlis Steinert, *Hitler's Krieg und die Deutschen: Stimmung und Haltung der Deutschen Bevölkerung im Zweiten Weltkrieg* (Düsseldorf, 1970), 564; Gerhard Boldt, *Hitler: The Last Ten Days* (New York, 1973) 115; George Stein, *To the Bitter End: The Waffen SS and the Defense of the Third Reich, 1943–1945* (New York, 1966), 224–227.

29 Stein, *To the Bitter End*, 293.

30 Hans Rumpf, *Das War der Bombenkrieg: Deutsche Städte im Feuersturm* (Oldenburg, 1961), 103–104.

31 Steinert, *Hitler's Krieg und die Deutschen*, 568–570.

32 Yehuda Bauer, "The Death Marches—January–May 1945," in *Contemporary Jewry: A Research Annual* (1983), 200.

33 Sebastian Haffner, "Voice of the Third Reich," *The Observer*, February 21, 1960.

34 *Reichsbevollmächtigter für den totalen Kriegseinsatz.*

35 *Reichsminister für Volksaufklärung und Propaganda.*

36 Peter Longerich, "Joseph Goebbels und der totale Krieg: Eine unbekannte Denkschrift des Propagandaministers vom 18, Juli 1944,"

Vierteljahrshefte für Zeitgeschichte, Vol.35, No.2 (1987), 289.

37 For example, the headline of *Der Spiegel* magazine from December 16, 2002, was "Hitler's Stalingrad: The Beginning of the End of the Third Reich."

38 Alan Bullock, "Preface," in Helmut Heiber (Ed.), *The Early Goebbels Diaries: The Journal of Joseph Goebbels from 1925–1926* (London, 1962), 10.

39 Otto Ohlendorf (1908–1951) was the commander of Einsatzgruppe D, which operated in the Soviet Union from June 1941 onward. He was tried and executed on June 8, 1951.

40 Roger Manvell and Heinrich Fraenkel, *Doctor Goebbels* (London, 1974), 10.

41 Robert Edwin Herzstein, *The War that Hitler Won: The Most Infamous Propaganda Campaign in History* (New York, 1978), 31; Kurt Ludecke, *I Knew Hitler* (London, 1938), 343.

42 Hermann Göring, Hitler's intended replacement, commander of the Luftwaffe—the German Air Force—served as the Minister President of Prussia and Commissioner of Aviation. Sentenced to be hanged during the Nuremberg trials, he committed suicide two hours before his execution.

43 Felix Möller, *The Film Minister: Goebbels and the Cinema in the "Third Reich"* (Stuttgart, 2000), 10.

44 Curt Riess, *Joseph Goebbels: Eine Biographie* (Baden-Baden, 1950), xi.

45 Erich Ebermayer and Hans-Otto Meissner, *Evil Genius: The Story of Joseph Goebbels* (London, 1953), 11–13; Riess, *Joseph Goebbels*, Chapter 1.

46 The battle of Verdun was fought in the months of February–December 1915, between the French and German armies. More than a million soldiers were killed. It was one of the bloodiest battles in World War I. Ebermayer and Meisser, *Evil Genius*, 19.

47 Ibid.

48 Joseph Goebbels, *Wilhelm von Schütz als Dramatiker. Ein Beitrag zur Geschichte des Dramatikers romantischen Stils,* Dissertation, Heidelberg, 1922. Von Schütz became famous in 1802, after the production of his play, *Lacrimas*.

49 For more on the subject, see Peter Longerich, *Goebbels: A Biography* (New York, 2015), chapter "The Rheydt Years."

50 Joseph Goebbels, *Michael: ein Deutsches Schicksal in Tagebuchblätern* (München, 1933), 5; Peter Gathmann und Martina Paul, *Narziss Goebbels: Eine psychohistorische Biografie* (Wien, 2009), 64–70.

51 Otto Strasser, a member of the Nazi party, gives his impression of the event: "to hear him, one would have supposed he had been a heroic figure in the Ruhr struggle, where he gave the impression that he had been imprisoned by the French and flogged daily in his cell." Ebermayer and Meissner, *Evil Genius*, 31–34; Otto Strasser, *Hitler and I* (London, 1940), 95.

52 Welch, *The Third Reich: Politics and Propaganda* (London, 1993), 12.

53 Herzstein, *The War that Hitler Won*, 39–40.

54 Gathmann und Paul, *Narziss Goebbels*, 27.

55 Strasser, *Hitler and I,* 83–84.

56 Ibid.

57 Goebbels, *Michael*, 32.

58 Richard Wagner (1813–1883) was a famous German composer. His philosophy and ideology, which contained anti-semitic ideas, influenced Hitler, who idolized him. According to Hitler's biographer Ian Kershaw "Hitler's passion for Wagner knew no bounds. A performance could affect him almost like a religious experience, plunging him into deep and mystical fantasies. Wagner amounted for him to the supreme artistic genius, the model to be emulated. Adolf was carried away by Wagner's powerful musical dramas, his evocation of a heroic, distant, and sublimely mystical Germanic past." Kershaw, *Hitler 1889–1936: Hubris* (New York, 2001).

59 The Valkyries (Walküre) were Nordic warrior women in Germanic mythology. They would take the warriors who fell in battle to Vallhala. It is also the name of the second part of Wagner's famous opera cycle, *The Ring of the Nibelungs (Der Ring des Nibelungen).*

60 Jeffrey Herf, *The Jewish Enemy: Nazi Propaganda during World War II and the Holocaust* (Cambridge, Mass, 2006), 21.

61 Ian Kershaw, *The "Hitler Myth." Image and Reality in the Third Reich* (Oxford, 1987), Chapter 1.

62 Goebbels, *Michael*, 31.

63 About designing the "Führer Myth" and strengthening Hitler's image by Goebbels, see Claus-Ekkehard Bärsch, *Erlösung und Vernichtung: Dr. phil. Joseph Goebbels: Zur Psyche und Ideologie eines jungen Nationalsozialisten* (München, 1987), 85–96.

64 Elke Fröhlich, "Hitler und Goebbels im Krisenjahr 1944: Aus den Tagebuchern des Reichspropagandaministers," *Vierteljahrshefte fur Zeitgeschichte* 38 (2) (1990), 201.

65 *TBJG*, July 23, 1944.

66 Ebermayer and Meissner, *Evil Genius*, 103–105.

67 *TBJG*, March 2, 1943.

68 At the beginning of 1943, Hitler established "the Committee of Three", composed of the three executive branches of the Führer's authority: the Wehrmacht's Supreme Command, the Reich's Chancellery, and the party's Chancellery. The goal of this body was to coordinate wartime policy. The committee only convened eleven times before dying out.

69 *TBJG*, March 8, 1945.

70 Martin Bormann (1900–1945), Hitler's secretary since 1943, one of the closest people to him and most zealous of the party's members. He dealt with internal affairs such as the *Aktion* T4 and the art

artifact robbery. His whereabouts after the war were unknown until 1998 when DNA testing confirmed that some human remains buried in 1945 were his.

71 Hugh Trevor-Roper (Ed.), *The Bormann Letters: The Private Correspondence between Martin Bormann and his Wife, from January 1943 to April 1945* (London, 1954), 146.

72 Rudolf Semmler, *Goebbels: The Man Next to Hitler* (London, 1947), 124. Semmler was a senior clerk at the Ministry of Public Enlightenment and Propaganda. At the recommendation of journalists from the Allied Forces, he kept a journal in which he detailed his relationship with Goebbels and what had happened there, from December 1940 to April 1945. He was captured by the Soviets, but first entrusted the journal to his wife, who got it published.

73 Manvell and Fraenkel, *Doctor Goebbels*, 199.

74 Ibid. See the research of Winfried Heinemann, *Operation "Valkyrie": A Military History of the 20 July 1944 Plot* (Berlin/Boston, 2022).

75 Manvell and Fraenkel, *Doctor Goebbels*, 124.

76 Kershaw, *Hitler 1936–1945: Nemesis* (London, 2000), 679. See also Albert Speer, *Erinnerungen* (Berlin, 1969), 393–394.

77 Anton Joachimsthaler, *The Last Days of Hitler: Legend, Evidence, and Truth* (London, 2000), 126. According to Gerhard Boldt, Hitler always saw Himmler as his most loyal confidant. See Gerhard Boldt, *Hitler: The*

Last Ten Days, 193. On April 13, 1945, Himmler said to Walter Schellenberg: "I believe that nothing more can be done with Hitler," and that he, Himmler, will try and find a way to finish "this business," that is, the war. See Walter Schellenberg, *The Schellenberg Memoirs* (London, 1965), 438–440.

78 Hans-Otto Meissner, *Magda Goebbels: A Biography* (London, 1980), 216.

79 *TBJG*, December 4, 1944.

80 Manvell and Fraenkel, *Doctor Goebbels*, 216.

81 No. 27, Rundfunkrede, July 26, 1944, in Helmut Heiber (Hrsg.), *Goebbels Reden 1939–1945*, Vol.2 (München, 1972), 342–343.

82 *TBJG*, July 26, 1944.

83 Longerich, "Joseph Goebbels und der Totale Krieg," 295.

84 Joseph Goebbels, "Die Fahne des Glaubnis," *Das Reich*, October 1, 1944.

85 Ibid, 292.

86 Semmler, *Goebbels*, 146–147.

87 Boelcke (Hrsg.), "Wollt ihr den totalen Krieg?" 312.

88 Heinz Linge, *Bis zum Untergang: Als Chef des Persönlichen Dienstes bei Hitler* (München, 1980), 237.

89 Kershaw, *Hitler 1936–1945: Nemesis*, 693.

90 Joachim Fest, *Hitler* (London, 1974), 735. Fest mentions ritualistic sacrifice for a reason. In the

last months of the war, it seemed that the Nazi leadership was overcome by a "pathological" obsession with death. Executions were routine in Germany at that time. An order was given that soldiers who deserted or failed to declare their faith in victory would be hanged. Goebbels and Bormann created martial kangaroo courts that sentenced people to be hanged almost at random, on charges of cowardice or treason. See Boldt, *Hitler: The Last Ten Days*, 160–161. The sanctity of life was gone, and death became trivial. German citizens who were lucky enough not to die in battle were often killed by their compatriots in squares, being informed on or falsely accused.

91 *TBJG*, July 23, 1944.

92 Elka Fröhlich claims that Goebbels needed to admire Hitler in order to give himself and his life meaning. See Fröhlich, "Hitler und Goebbels," 209.

93 Fest, *Hitler*, 739.

94 Kershaw, *Hitler 1936–1945: Nemesis*, 579.

95 *TBJG*, August 3, 1944.

96 Nicolaus von Below, *At Hitler's Side: The Memoirs of Hitler's Luftwaffe Adjutant 1937–1945* (London, 2001), 224.

97 *TBJG*, July 23, 1944.

98 Goebbels, "Kraft und Einsicht des Volkes," *Das Reich*, January 7, 1945.

99 Hancock, *The National Socialist Leadership*, 165.

100 Goebbels, "Der Glaube entscheidt," *Völkischer Beobachte*r, May 25, 1944.

101 Goebbels, 'Widerstand um jeden Preis," *Das Reich*, April 22, 1945.

102 Trevor-Roper (Ed.), *The Bormann Letters*, 77. Semmler says that on January 12, 1945, during a visit by Hitler to the Goebbels household, he handed Goebbels's wife Magda a bouquet of roses and explained they were the best he could find, since her husband had closed down all the flower shops in Berlin. Semmler, Goebbels, 174. At the Goebbels's house there was a ten-meter-deep cellar that went underground, which was where they would go during bombardments. The cellar was organized and decorated and had a shower and beds in it. Under those conditions, it was rather difficult to understand what millions of German citizens were going through in their own shelters. Meissner, *Magda Goebbels*, 225.

103 Hancock, *The National Socialist Leadership*, 153.

104 Semmler, *Goebbels*, 194.

105 Helmut Heiber (Hrsg.), *Lagebesprechungen im Führerhauptquartier: Protokollfragmente aus Hitlers militärischen Konferenzen 1942–1945* (München, 1963), 245, July 23, 1944.

106 Manvell and Fraenkel, *Doctor Goebbels*, 223.

107 Boldt, *Hitler: The Last Ten Days*, 160.

108 Semmler, *Goebbels*, 177.

109 Linge, *Bis zum Untergang*, 242.

110 Kershaw, *Hitler 1936–1945: Nemesis*, 554.

111 Fest, *Hitler*, 758.

112 Goldensohn, *The Nuremberg Interviews*, 112.

113 Helmut Heiber, *Goebbels: A Biography* (New York, 1972), 334.

114 Semmler, *Goebbels*, 181.

115 Heiber, *Goebbels: A Biography, 322.*

116 *TBJG*, March 15, 1945.

117 On September 1, 1944, Bormann wrote to his wife of his concern for Hitler. He said that "The Führer... lives down in his dugout, has only electric light, only the stale air of the dugout—where pressure is always too high because fresh air has to be pumped in—and it is just as if he were living in a cellar without any light. Life in such a concrete box is, after all, unhealthy, and in the long run quite unbearable for any living being. Any normal plant would die off because of the lack of air, light, and an atmosphere of life," See: Trevor-Roper (Ed.), *The Bormann Letters*, 129.

118 Manvell and Fraenkel, *Doctor Goebbels*, 202.

119 Reichsprogramm, "Dr. Goebbels in Görlitz," March 11, 1945.

120 In March 1940, Joseph Stalin ordered mass executions of Polish soldiers and officers captured by the Soviet Union. The Bodies of over 20,000 of them were found in April, 1943, by Wehrmacht soldiers.

121 *TBJG*, April 14, 1943.

122 Semmler, *Goebbels*, 83.

123 Meissner, *Magda Goebbels*, 303 (Nein, nein, mein Lieber, im Katyn, das waren tatsächlich die Russen. Unsere Massengräber dürften wo anders liegen).

124 Helmut Heiber, *Goebbels: A Biography*, 343.

125 Goebbels, "Die Urheber des Unglücks der Welt," *Das Reich*, January 1, 1945. And also in his speech at Hitler's last birthday, on April 19, 1945: "Once again the enemy forces are storming our defence lines. Behind them, the International Jewry holds the whip. It does not want peace and will not rest until it achieves its infernal goal of global destruction." See Joseph Goebbels: "Rundfunkansprache am Vorabend von Hitlers 56. Geburtstag," in Heiber (Hrsg.), *Goebbels Reden*, No.31, 452.

126 Semmler, *Goebbels*, 98.

127 *TBJG*, March 2, 1943.

128 *TBJG*, March 14, 1945.

129 *TBJG*, March 4, 1944.

130 *TBJG*, March 2, 1943.

131 Goebbels, *Michael*, 122 (Durch Opfer zur Erlösung!).

132 Meissner, *Magda Goebbels*, 233--234.

133 Riess, *Joseph Goebbels*, 438–439. In this context, what Goebbels had written in Michael seems rather ironic: "How can one write books and gather

information while the Reich lies in ruins?" See Goebbels, *Michael*, 121.

134 Riess, *Joseph Goebbels*, 474.

135 Boldt, *Hitler: The Last Ten Days*, 147; Fest, *Hitler*, 738; Manvell and Fraenkel, *Doctor Goebbels*, 280.

136 Meissner, *Magda Goebbels*, 241–242.

137 Ibid; Longerich, *Goebbels,* 682–683.

138 Ebermayer and Meissner, *Evil Genius*, 78.

139 Manvell and Fraenkel, *Doctor Goebbels*, 247.

140 Boldt, *Hitler: The Last Ten Days*, 165. Goebbels was attached to his children. Frau K, their nanny, said that when he was in the presence of his children, Goebbels would change. The atmosphere would lighten, and he seemed to be unburdened. He was calm and cheerful, his children were ideal in his eyes. They only had one flaw: they were, he thought, too well mannered. He wanted them to be wilder. He would go out of his way to taunt them and would be delighted every time one of them talked back to him. See Meissner, *Magda Goebbels*, 245.

141 Horst Wessel was born in 1907. He was immortalized in the motion picture based on his biography, *Hans Westmar. Einer von vielen,* released in 1933. The character of Hans Westmar, the hero, was represented as the ideal SA man and an Aryan god.

142 Semmler, *Goebbles*, 187.

143 Boldt, *Hitler: The Last Ten Days*, 116.

144 Goebbels, *Michael*, 201 ("Viele sterben zu spät und einige zu früh. Noch klingt fremd die Lehre: stirb zur rechten Zeit!").

145 Herzstein, *The War that Hitler Won*, 48.

146 Joachim Fest, *Inside Hitler's Bunker* (New York, 2004), 774.

147 Thymian Bussemer, "'Über Propaganda zu Diskutieren, hat wenig Zweck': Zur Medien- und Propagandapolitik von Joseph Goebbels," in Lutz Hachmeister und Michael Kloft (Hrsg.), *Das Goebbels-Experiment: Propaganda und Politik* (München, 2005), 50.

148 Ernst Bramsted, *Goebbels and National Socialist Propaganda, 1925–45* (Michigan, 1965), xix.

149 Clemens Zimmermann, "From Propaganda to Modernization: Media Policy and Media Audiences under National Socialism," *German History* 24 (3) (2006), 433.

150 Victor Klemperer, *The Language of the Third Reich: LTI, Lingua Tertii Imperii: A Philologist's Notebook* (London, 2000), 15–16. The word *fanaticism* comes from the Latin word *fanum*, meaning shrine or palace. The word *fanatic* was used to describe someone who is in a religious ecstasy.

151 Viktor Klemperer, *I Will Bear Witness, 1942–1945* (New York, 2001), February 27, 1943.

152 Ernst Hans Gombrich, *Myth and Reality in German War-Time Broadcasts* (London, 1970), 14.

153 Gustave Le Bon, *The Crowd: A Study of the Popular Mind* (New York, 1972), 106.

154 Theodor W. Adorno, "Freudian Theory and the Pattern of Fascist Propaganda," from Michael Mey-Dan and Avraham Yasur (Eds.), *Frankfurt School: A Collection* (Tel Aviv, 2003), 241.

155 Elias Canetti, *Crowds and Power* (New York, 1966), 40.

156 William McDougall, *The Group Mind* (Cambridge, 1920), 45.

157 Robert Jay Lifton, *Thought Reform and the Psychology of Totalism: A Study of "Brainwashing" in China* (New York, 1961), 420–421.

158 Goebbels's diary from August 9, 1932, quoted in Stefan Krings, "Das Propagandaministerium: Joseph Goebbels und seine Spezialisten," in Hachmeister und Kloft (Hrsg.), *Das Goebbels-Experiment: Propaganda und Politik*, 29.

159 Derrick Sington and Arthur Weidenfeld, *The Goebbels Experiment: A Study of the Nazi Propaganda Machine* (New Haven, 1944), 75.

160 Willi Boelcke (Hrsg.), *Kriegspropaganda, 1939–1941: Geheime Ministerkonferenzen im Reichspropagandaministerium* (Stuttgart, 1966), vii–viii.

161 Hans Schwarz van Berk, "Vorwort: Von der Kunst, zur Welt zu sprechen," in *Die Zeit ohne Beispiel: Reden und Aufsätze aus dem Jahren 1939/40/41* (München, 1941), 9–13; Norbert Frei und Johannes Schmitz,

Journalismus im Dritten Reich (München, 1989), 168–173.

162 Schwarz van Berk, "Vorwort: Von der Kunst".

163 Goebbels's speech from June 19, 1935, quoted in Schmitz-Berning, *Vokabular des National-Sozialismus* (Berlin, 2000), 479.

164 Werner Stephan, *Joseph Goebbels: Dämon einer Diktatur* (Stuttgart, 1949), 44. This opinion was also shared by Gombrich, in Myth and Reality, 3.

165 Riess, *Joseph Goebbels*, 336.

166 Bussemer, "Über Propaganda zu Diskutieren," 52.

167 Michael Balfour, *Propaganda in War 1939–1945: Organisations, Policies, and Publics in Britain and Germany* (London, 1979), 31.

168 Z.A.B. Zeman, *Nazi Propaganda* (London, 1966), 43.

169 Goebbels, *Vom Kaiserhof zur Reichskanzlei*, 17. On the Jews' central position in the German press, see Saul Friedländer, *Nazi Germany and the Jews: Prosecution Years, 1933–1939* (New York, 1997), Chapter 3: "Redemptive Anti-semitism."

170 Christian Härtel, "'Soldat unter Soldaten:' Der Journalist Joseph Goebbels," in: Hachmeister und Kloft (Hrsg.), *Das Goebbels-Experiment: Propaganda und Politik*, 16.

171 Herf, *The Jewish Enemy*, 26–27; "Völkischer Beobachter," *in Enzyklopädie des Nationalsozialismus*, 784–785.

172 Russel Lemmons, *Goebbels and Der Angriff* (Lexington, Kentucky, 1994), 111–112.

173 Quoted in Härtel, "Soldat unter Soldaten," 19.

174 Lemmons, *Goebbels and Der Angriff*, 37.

175 Karl Dietrich Bracher, *The German Dictatorship: Roots, Structure, and Outcomes of National Socialism* (New York, 1971), 134–135.

176 "Der Angriff," in Wolfgang Benz, Hermann Graml, and Hermann Weiss (Hrsg.), *Enzyklopädie des Nationalsozialismus* (Stuttgart, 1998), 362; Frei und Schmitz, *Journalismus im Dritten Reich*, 97.

177 Frei und Schmitz, *Journalismus im Dritten Reich*, 108–110. The Jewish literary critic, Marcel Reich-Ranicki, says that while he was at his hideout in Warsaw, Poland, he quickly became an avid reader of the newspaper *Das Reich*: "I mostly read the culture section of the Reich. I must admit, I not only read it, but rather enjoyed it," he wrote. See the memoirs of Marcel Reich-Ranicki, *Mein Leben* (Stuttgart, 2000).

178 Alfred Klemmt, "Friedrich Nietzsche: Zum 100. Geburstag am 15. Oktober," *Das Reich*, October 8, 1944.

179 Frei und Schmitz, *Journalismus im Dritten Reich*, 101–102.

180 Julius Streicher (1885–1946) was a radical anti-Semite, editor, and writer in the anti-Semitic journal *Der Stürmer*, which he founded in 1923. He was executed by hanging in Nuremberg on October 16, 1946. He devoted his life

to researching the Jews and, according to his own words, became an expert on Jewish literature and built an entire library of it. "Anti-Semitism is an entirely dignified and understood position," he claimed. He wanted to become an authority on anti-Semitism. See his interview in Goldenshon, *Nuremberg* 1946, 254.

181 Frei und Schmitz, *Journalismus im Dritten Reich*, 104–107.

182 Herf, *The Jewish Enemy*, 140.

183 Frei und Schmitz, *Journalismus im Dritten Reich*, 30.

184 Walther Funk was born in Königsberg, Eastern Prussia. From 1916, he was a writer and editor of various newspapers. He worked at the Department of Propaganda until 1937. From that year until 1945 he served as Chief Plenipotentiary for Economics after replacing Hjalmar Schacht. He was given a life sentence at the Nuremberg trials and was released in 1957 for health issues.

185 See Goldenshon, *Nuremberg 1946*.

186 Balfour, *Propaganda in War*, 20.

187 Fritsche was born in Bochum, Westphalia, in 1900. He began his career as the editor of the "Prussian Yearbook." He was tried at Nuremberg and was found not guilty. He was later tried again and sentenced to nine years in prison. He died of cancer in Cologne, in September 1953. Fritsche was close to his mother, and he would say about her: "Mother did not like Goebbels at all. She only met him once, when he visited me at my office. I do not know why

she despised him so much. He was nice and polite to her, but she told me afterwards that I had to be free of him. She said he was a small man, and I was a big man and that Goebbels wanted to misuse me," Goldenshon, *Nuremberg, 1946,* 51.

188 Gombrich, *Myth and Reality*, 5; Welch, *The Third Reich*, 30.

189 Walch, *The Third Reich*, 30–33.

190 Friedländer, *Nazi Germany and the Jew*, Chapter 1.

191 We should mention in this regard the famous essay by Richard Wagner, "Judaism in Music" (*Das Judentum in der Musik*). In a book published in 1935 by the Institute for Study of the Jewish Question, headed by Alfred Rosenberg and funded by the Nazi party, the "artistic atrophy" of the Jews is detailed in all cultural fields: literature, music, cinema, fine arts, etc. See: *Die Juden in Deutschland* (München, 1935). On the first page of this book, there is a section from Goebbels's speech at the Party Day in Nuremberg, 1933, in which he said: "It is not that we have turned the Jews into the main and sole defendants of the German spiritual and economic catastrophe. We acknowledge all the other reasons that led to the sinking of our people. But we are brave enough to acknowledge their role in this process and name it."

192 Trevor-Roper (Ed.), *The Bormann Letters*, 173, February 15, 1945.

193 David Weinberg, "Approaches to the Study of Film in the Third Reich: A Critical Appraisal," *Journal of Contemporary History* 19 (1) (1984), 107–110.

194 On Goebbels's part in planning the Kristallnacht, see Stefan Kley, "Hitler and the Pogrom of November 9/10, 1938," *Yad Vashem Studies* 28 (1999). The author claims that, at that time, Goebbels's status as a minister was undermined due to the incident with Lida Baarova, the Czech actress with whom he had an affair that led to a crisis in his marriage. Hitler himself got involved in favor of the Goebbels marriage, but resented Joseph because of it. Klay claims that arranging the pogrom was a means of invoking the Führer's trust once again.

195 Stig Hornshoj-Moller and David Culbert, "'Der Ewige Jude' (1940): Joseph Goebbels's Unequaled Monument to Antisemitism," *Historical Journal of Film, Radio and Television* 12 (1) (1992), 41–42.

196 *TBJG*, November 6, 1936.

197 Franz-Josef Heyen (Hrsg.), *Parole der Woche: Eine Wandzeitung im Dritten Reich, 1936–1943* (München, 1983), 7–10.

198 Quoted in Daniel Uziel, "Wehrmacht and the Jews Propaganda Battalions," *Yad Vashem Studies* 29 (2000), 28. It is known that executions of Jews were also photographed for archiving and documentation.

199 Leonard Doob, "Goebbels's Principles of Propaganda," in Robert Jackall (Ed.), *Propaganda* (New York, 1995), 193.

200 Ebermayer and Meissner, *Evil Genius*, 214.

201 Schwarz van Berk, "Vorwort: Von der Kunst, zur Welt zu sprechen."

202 Baird, *The Mythical World*, 17.

203 Boelcke, *Kriegspropaganda*, xvii. According to le Bon, the crowd never chased the truth and turned their backs on proof when it did not suit them. They would rather worship a lie if it enticed them, and whoever tried to ruin their illusions would become their victim. The crowd is not influenced by logic, which is why good speakers will always address the crowd's feelings and never their logic. See Le Bon, *The Crowd*, 110–112.

204 Semmler, *Goebbels*, 163.

205 Boelcke, *Kriegspropaganda*, January 4, 1943, 313.

206 *TBJG*, March 14, 1945.

207 Joseph Goebbels, "Der Krieg und die Juden," in *Der steile Aufstieg*, 263–270.

208 Goebbels, "Nun, Volk, steh auf, und Sturm brich los! Rede im Berliner Sportpalast."

209 *TBJG*, March 9, 1943; Boelcke, *Kriegspropaganda*, February 20, 1943, 334.

210 Baird, *The Mythical World*, 198. It should be mentioned, that among the victims of the Soviets in Katyn, there were also over 400 Jews who served in the Polish Army.

211 Herf, *The Jewish Enemy*, 96--97.

212 Goebbels, "Der Krieg und die Juden."

213 *TBJG*, May 8, 1943.

214 Joseph Goebbels, "Die Juden sind schuld!" November 16, 1941, in *Das eherne Herz: Reden und Aufsätze aus den Jahren 1941/42* (München, 1943), 85–91.

215 Joseph Goebbels, "Mimikry," July 20, 1941, in *Die Zeit ohne Beispiel*, 526–531.

216 Goebbels, "Die Juden sind schuld!"

217 Adolf Hitler, *Mein Kampf* (München, 1939), 334. More on the use made by the Nazis of the word *parasit* and the adjective *parasitär*, see Schmitz-Berning, *Vokabular des National-Sozialismus*, 460–464.

218 Frei und Schmitz, *Journalismus im Dritten Reich*, 117.

219 *TBJG*, April 18, 1943.

220 Bramsted, *Goebbels and National Socialist Propaganda,* 398. According to Klemperer, in LTI, the language of the Third Reich, the word *Ausrotten* meant not only annihilating, but also an annihilation that should be zealously achieved. See Klemperer, *The Language of the Third Reich.*

221 Goebbels, "Die Juden sind Schuld!"

222 Semmler, *Goebbels*, 63–64.

223 Baird, *The Mythical World*, 40.

224 Kotze und Krausnick, "*Es Spricht der Führer,*" 367.

225 Schmitz-Berning, *Vokabular des National-Sozialismus,* 228–229.

226 Joseph Goebbels, "Der Blick nach vorne," January 31, 1943, in: *Der steile Aufstieg: Reden und Aufsätze aus den Jahren 1942/43* (Leipzig, 1944), 151–158.

227 Joseph Goebbels, "Nun, Volk, steh auf, und Sturm brich los!" Rede im Berliner Sportpalast, February 18, 1943, in *Der steile Aufstieg*, 167–204.

228 Gunter Moltmann, "Goebbels's Rede zum Totalen Krieg am 18. Februar 1943," *Vierteljahrshefte für Zeitgeschichte* 12 (1) (1964), 42.

229 Welch, *The Third Reich*, 121.

230 Quoted in Weinberg, "Approaches to the Study of Film," 114.

231 Jeffrey Herf, "The 'Jewish War': Goebbels and the Antisemitic Campaigns of the Nazi Propaganda Ministry," *Holocaust and Genocide Studies* 19 (1) (2005), 53.

232 Lifton, *Thought Reform*, 423.

233 Gerald Kirwin, "Waiting for Retaliation: A Study in Nazi Propaganda Behavior and German Civilian Morale," *Journal of Contemporary History* 16 (1981), 565–566.

234 Krings, "Das Propagandaministerium," 33.

235 Kirwin, "Waiting for Retaliation," 567–568. Goebbels asked the Wehrmacht authorities to give titles "that will stir an emotional effect," and so the names "Hell Hounds" (*Höllenhund*) and "Storm Birds" (*Sturmvogel*) were suggested.

236 Welch, *The Third Reich*, 114.

237 Baird, *The Mythical World*, 225.

238 Meissner, *Magda Goebbels*, 217.

239 Joseph Goebbels, "Die Bilder der erschlagenen Kinder unsere ständigen Wegbegleiter," *Völkischer Beobachter*, March 13, 1945.

240 *TBJG*, March 9, 1945.

241 Alastair Noble, "The People's Levy—The Volkssturm and Popular Mobilization in Eastern Germany, 1944–45," *The Journal of Strategic Studies* Vol. 24 (1) (2001), 172.

242 Semmler, *Goebbels*, 175.

243 The meaning of the word *Wolf* is the same as in English, and according to old Germanic folklore, a man wearing a wolf skin becomes the vicious animal itself in moments of madness and ecstasy. The first *Werwolf* movement in Germany was a Romantic one in the fourteenth century. On the origins of the ritual of turning a man into a wolf and its place in Germanic Mythology, see Robert Eisler, *Man into Wolf: An Anthropological Interpretation of Sadism, Masochism and Lycanthropy* (Santa Barbara, 1978).

244 Baird, *The Mythical World*, 218.

245 Joseph Goebbels, "Widerstand um jeden Preis," *Das Reich*, April 22, 1945.

246 *TBJG*, March 20, 1945.

247 Trevor-Roper (Ed.), *The Bormann Letters*, 197–198. According to folklore, the Nibelungs who fought

the Huns refused to surrender and fought to the last man, faithful to their leader.

248 Rudolf Höss, *The Auschwitz Commandant Testifies: Notes from Rudolf Ferdinand Höss* (New York, 1961).

249 Kershaw, *Hitler 1936–1945: Nemesis, 554.*

250 Wilhelm Deist, "The Road to Ideological War: Germany 1918–1945," in Murry Williamson, Macgregor Knox, and Alvin Bernstein (Eds.), *The Making of Strategy: Rulers, States, and War* (Cambridge, New York, 1994), 390–391.

251 *TBJG,* April 4, 1945.

252 Baird, *To Die for Germany,* 240.

253 Hitler's speech from April 16, 1945. See Max Domarus (Hrsg.), *Hitler Reden und Proklamationen,* 1932–1945 (München, 1965), 223.

254 H.R. Trevor-Roper, *Hilter's Last Days* (London, 1978).

255 Fest, *Hitler.* See the chapter "Götterdämmerung," also Paul Massing, *Rehearsal for Destruction: A Study of Political Anti-Semitism in Imperial Germany* (New York, 1949), 39–40.

256 Reimer Hansen, *Das Ende des Dritten Reiches: Die deutsche Kapitulation 1945* (Stuttgart, 1966), 40; Joachimsthaler, *The Last Days of Hitler,* 91. According to Wegner, the hopeful thesis for a divide or tear between the Allied forces does not sit well with the facts, since the Nazi theory believed that the Jews were behind each of them and so they will not disarm themselves. See Bernd Wegner, "Hitler,

der Zweite Weltkrieg und die Choreographie des Untergangs," *Geschichte und Gesellschaft* 26 (3) (2000), 497.

257 *TBJG*, March 5, 1945.

258 Joachimsthaler, *The Last Days of Hitler*, 92.

259 Hansen, *Das Ende des Dritten Reiches*, 49–50.

260 Manvell and Fraenkel, *Doctor Goebbels*, 248.

261 Hansen, *Das Ende des Dritten Reiches*, 66–68.

262 Manvell and Fraenkel, *Doctor Goebbels*, 237–238.

263 Fest, *Inside Hitler's Bunker*, 143-158.

264 Raul Hilberg "Auschwitz and the Final solution" in Yisrael Gutman and Michael Berenbaum (Eds.) *Anatomy of the Auschwitz Death Camp* (Bloomington, 1994), 81–92.

265 Livia Rothkirchen "The 'Final Solution' in Its Last Stages," *Yad Vashem Studies* 8 (1971), 13.

266 Walter Laqueur, "Auschwitz," in Michael Neufeld and Michael Berenbaum (Eds.), *The Bombing of Auschwitz: Should the Allies have Attempted it?* (New York, 2000), 189–190.

267 Robert Gellately, *Backing Hitler: Consent and Coercion in Nazi Germany* (Oxford, 2001), 236–241.

268 Bauer, "The Death Marches January–May 1945," 199–200.

269 Paul Weindling, "From Medical War Crimes to Compensation: The Plight of the Victims of Human

Experiments," in Wolfgang Eckart (Ed.), *Man, Medicine, and the State: The Human Body as an Object of Government Sponsored Medical Research in the 20th Century* (Stuttgart, 2006), 245.

270 Leni Yahil, *The Holocaust*, 449–450.

271 Robert Jan van Pelt, "*A Site in Search of a Mission*," in Gutman and Berenbaum (Eds.), *Anatomy of the Auschwitz Death Camp*, 93-156.

272 It should be mentioned that van den Bruck did not wait to see whether the revolution he preached would come true, as he committed suicide in Berlin on May 30, 1925, at the age of 49, after a nervous breakdown.

273 Julius Langbehn, *Rembrandt als Erzieher* (1890).

274 Stern, *The Politics of Cultural Despair*, 131–32; George Mosse, *The Crisis of German Ideology: Intellectual Origins of the Third Reich* (New York, 1981), 39–44.

275 Stern, *The Politics of Cultural Despair*, 185–186.

276 Eugen Dühring, *Die Judenfrage als Racen-, Sitten-, und Culturfrage* (1880).

277 Mosse, *The Crisis of German Ideology*, 131.

278 Friedländer, *Nazi Germany and the Jews*, 74.

279 Jehuda Wallach, *The Dogma of the Battle of Annihilation: The Theories of Clausewitz and Schlieffen and their Impact on the German Conduct of Two World Wars* (Westport, Connecticut, 1986), 242.

280 Weiss, *The Ideology of Death*, 132–133.

281 Jennifer Michael Hecht, "Vacher de Lapouge and the Rise of Nazi Science," *Journal of the History of Ideas* (2000), 285–290.

282 Dietrich Eckart, *The Bolshevism from Moses to Lenin: A Dialogue between Hitler and Myself.*

283 Hartmut Zelinsky, "Decay, annihilation, world rapture," *Zmanim: A History Quarterly* 79 (Summer 2002), 43.

284 Friedländer, *Nazi Germany and the Jews*, 89-90.

285 Arthur de Gobineau, *Essai sur l'inégalité des races humaines* (1853–1855).

286 Paul Laurence Rose, *Wagner: Race and Revolution* (New Haven, 1992), 139. On developing the race theories of Chamberlain and de Gobineau, see Georg Lukács, *Die Zerstörung der Vernunft* (Neuwied, 1962), 579–591, 605–621.

287 Erich Goldhagen, "Obsession and Realpolitik in the 'Final Solution,'" *Patterns of Prejudice* 12 (1) (1978), 5.

288 Boaz Neumann, *Nazi World View: Space-Body-Language* (Tel Aviv, 2002), 169. For further discussion on the Jewish "stereotypical body" as opposed to the Aryan one, as perceived by the Nazis, see Neumann's book, 218–228.

289 Richard Wagner, *Judaism in Music.*

290 Zelinsky, "Decay, Annihilation, World Rapture," 39.

291 Wagner, *Judaism in Music*. By using the name Ahasuerus, a distortion of the name of the Persian king Xerxes I, Wagner refers to the legend of the

"Eternal Jew." See Paul Laurence Rose, *German Question, Jewish Question, Revolutionary Antisemitism: From Kant to Wagner* (Princeton, 1990), 23–24.

292 Hitler, *Mein Kampf*, Chapter 10.

293 *TBJG*, March 2, 1943.

294 Wegner, "Hitler, der Zweite Weltkrieg und die Choreographie des Untergangs," 506–507.

295 *TBJG*, March 5, 1945.

296 Hans Mommsen, "There was no Führer Order," in Donald Niewyk (Ed.), *The Holocaust: Problems and Perspectives of Interpretation* (Boston, 1997), 36–38.

297 Hannah Arendt, *Eichmann in Jerusalem: A Report on the Banality of Evil* (London, 1963), see the chapter "The Wannsee Conference, or Pontius Pilate."

298 Rüdiger Övermanns, *Deutsche militärische Verluste im Zweiten Weltkrieg* (München, 2000), 238–239.

299 Deist, "The Road to Ideological War," 380–385. See also Eberhard Jäckel, *Hitler's World View* (Cambridge, 1995), especially the chapter "The Outlines of Foreign Policy."

300 Goebbels, "Die Juden sind Schuld!"

301 Quoted in: Broszat, "Hitler and the Beginning of the Final Solution," 78.

302 Operation T4 received its name from the location of the office on Tiergartenstraße no. 4 in Berlin, where preparations were made for Operation Euthanasia in the summer of 1939. The operation

was part of a plan to renew the German people's "racial hygiene." We can also see the gradual escalation of the plan here: on July 14, 1933, the "Hereditary Offspring Rejection Law" was passed, meaning the forced sterilization of the mentally ill or developmentally challenged people, and people with other disabilities. In February 1939, the Nazi regime started killing children in special education institutes. On September 1, 1939—the day the war started—Hitler signed the Euthanasia Order, and in December of that year they started killing patients in gas trucks.

303 Mommsen, "There was no Führer Order," 31.

304 Karl Binding und Alfred Hoche, *Die Freigabe der Vernichtung lebensunwerten Lebens* (Leipzig, 1922).

305 Robert Proctor, "Nazi Medicine and the Politics of Knowledge," in Sandra Harding (Ed.), *The Racial Economy of Science: Toward a Democratic Future* (Bloomington, Indiana, 1993), 349.

306 *TBJG*, April 18, 1944.

307 Speer, *Erinnerungen*, 275.

308 Oswald Spengler, *Der Untergang des Abendlandes: Umrisse Einer Morphologie der Weltgeschichte* (München, 1923).

309 *TBJG*, March 22, 1945.

310 Heiber (Hrsg.), *Goebbels Reden*, no. 29, Köln, Werkhalle eines Industriebetriebs—Kundgebung

des Gaues Köln—Aachen der NSDAP, October 3, 1944, 407.

311 Ibid, 408–409.

312 Joachim Fest, *The Face of the Third Reich* (New York, 1970), "Joseph Goebbels."

313 Sebastian Haffner, "Voice of the Third Reich," *The Observer*, February 21, 1960.

BIBLIOGRAPHY

Diaries

Fröhlich, Elke (Hrsg.), *Die Tagebücher von Joseph Goebbels*, München, 1987–1996.

Heiber, Helmut (Ed.), *The Early Goebbels Diaries: The Journal of Joseph Goebbels from 1925–1926*, London, 1962.

Hochhuth, Rolf (Hrsg.), *Joseph Goebbels: Tagebücher 1945: Die Letzten Aufzeichnungen*, Hamburg, 1977.

Lochner, Louis P., *The Goebbels Diaries*, New York, 1948.

Writings and Speeches

Goebbels, Joseph, *Michael: Ein Deutsches Schicksal in Tagebuchblättern*, München, 1934.

Goebbels, Joseph, *Vom Kaiserhof zur Reichskanzlei: Eine historische Darstellung in Tagebuchblättern*, München, 1934.

Goebbels, Joseph, *Die Zeit ohne Beispiel: Reden und Aufsätze aus den Jahren 1939–41*, München, 1941.

Goebbels, Joseph, *Das eherne Herz: Reden und Aufsätze aus den Jahren 1941–42*, München, 1943.

Goebbels, Joseph, *Der steile Aufstieg: Reden und Aufsätze aus den Jahren 1942–43*, Leipzig, 1944.

Heiber, Helmut (Hrsg.), *Goebbels Reden 1939–1945*, München, 1972.

Primary Publications

Schwarz van Berk, Hans, "Vorwort: Von der Kunst, zur Welt zu sprechen," in *Die Zeit ohne Beispiel: Reden und Aufsätze aus dem Jahren 1939–41*, München, 1941, 9–13.

Binding, Karl und Alfred Hoche, *Die Freigabe der Vernichtung lebensunwerten Lebens*, Leipzig, 1922.

Boelcke, Willi (Hrsg.), *Kriegspropaganda, 1939–1941: Geheime Ministerkonferenzen im Reichspropagandaministerium*, Stuttgart, 1966.

Boelcke, Willi (Hrsg.), *"Wollt ihr den totalen Krieg?": Die geheime Goebbels- Konferenzen, 1939–1943*, München, 1969.

Canetti, Elias, *Crowds and Power*, New York, 1966.

Domarus, Max (Hrsg.), *Hitler Reden und Proklamationen, 1932–1945*, München, 1965.

Fehst, Herman, *Bolschewismus und Judentum: Das jüdische Element in der Führerschaft des Bolschewismus*, Berlin, 1934.

Heiber, Helmut (Hrsg.), *Lagebesprechungen im Führerhauptquartier: Protokollfragmente aus Hitlers militärischen Konferenzen 1942–1945*, München, 1963.

Höss, Rudolf, *The Auschwitz Commandant Testifies: Notes from Rudolf Ferdinand Höss*, New York, 1961

Kotze, Hildegard von und Helmut Krausnick (Hrsg.), *"Es Spricht der Führer": 7 Exemplarische Hitler-Reden*, Gütersloh, 1966.

Le Bon, Gustave, *The Crowd: A Study of the Popular Mind*, New York, 1972.

Ludecke, Kurt, *I Knew Hitler*, London, 1938.

McDougall, William, *The Group Mind*, Cambridge, 1920.

Spengler, Oswald, *Der Untergang des Abendlandes: Umrisse Einer Morphologie der Weltgeschichte*, München, 1923.

Strasser, Otto, *Hitler and I*, London, 1940.

Trevor-Roper, Hugh (Ed.), *The Bormann Letters: The Private Correspondence between Martin Bormann and his Wife, from January 1943 to April 1945*, London, 1954.

Die Juden in Deutschland, Herausgegeben von Institut zum Studium der Judenfrage, München, 1935.

Goebbels Biographies

Bärsch, Claus-Ekkehard, *Erlösung und Vernichtung: Dr. phil. Joseph Goebbels zur Psyche und Ideologie eines jungen Nationalsozialisten 1923–1927*, München, 1987.

Bramsted, Ernst, *Goebbels and National Socialist Propaganda, 1925–1945*, Michigan, 1965.

Ebermayer, Erich and Hans-Otto Meissner, *Evil Genius: The Story of Joseph Goebbels*, London, 1953.

Gathmann, Peter und Martina Paul, *Narziss Goebbels: Eine psychohistorische Biografie*, Wien, 2009.

Heiber, Helmut, *Goebbels*, New York, 1972.

Lemmons, Russel, *Goebbels and Der Angriff*, Lexington, Kentucky, 1994.

Manvell, Roger and Heinrich Fraenkel, *Doctor Goebbels*, London, 1974.

Meissner, Hans-Otto, *Magda Goebbels: A Biography*, London, 1980.

Möller, Felix, *The Film Minister: Goebbels and the Cinema in the "Third Reich,"* Stuttgart, 2000.

Oven, Wilfred von, *Mit Goebbels bis zum Ende*, Buenos Aires, 1949.

Reimann, Viktor, *The Man who Created Hitler: Joseph Goebbels*, London, 1977.

Riess, Curt, *Joseph Goebbels: Eine Biographie*, Zürich, 1949.

Semmler, Rudolf, *Goebbels: The Man Next to Hitler*, London, 1947.

Sington, Derrick and Arthur Weidenfeld, *The Goebbels Experiment: A Study of the Nazi Propaganda Machine*, New Haven, 1944.

Stephan, Werner, *Joseph Goebbels: Dämon einer Diktatur*, Stuttgart, 1949.

Additional Sources

Adorno, Theodor W., "Freudian Theory and the Pattern of Fascist Propaganda," from: Michael Mey-Dan and Avraham Yasur (Eds.), *Frankfurt School: A Collection*, Tel Aviv, 2003.

Arendt, Hannah, *Eichmann in Jerusalem: A Report on the Banality of Evil*, London, 1963.

Baird, Jay, *The Mythical World of Nazi Propaganda, 1939–1945*, Minneapolis, 1974.

Balfour, Michael, *Propaganda in War 1939–1945: Organisations, Policies, and Publics in Britain and Germany*, London, 1979.

Bauer, Yehuda, "The Death Marches January–May 1945," in *Contemporary Jewry: A Research Annual*, 1983, 199–221.

Below, Nicolaus von, *At Hitler's Side: The Memoirs of Hitler's Luftwaffe Adjutant 1937–1945*, London, 2001.

Benz, Wolfgang, Hermann Graml und Hermann Weiss (Hrsg.), *Enzyklopädie des Nationalsozialismus*, Stuttgart, 1998.

Boldt, Gerhard, *Hitler: The Last Ten Days*, New York, 1973.

Bracher, Karl Dietrich, *The German Dictatorship: Roots, Structure, and Outcomes of National Socialism*, New York, 1971.

Broszat, Martin, "Hitler and the Genesis of the 'Final Solution': An Assessment of David Irving's Theses." *Yad Vashem Studies* 13, 1980, 61–98.

Browning, Christopher, *The Origins of the Final Solution: The Evolution of Nazi Jewish Policy, September 1939–March 1942,* Jerusalem, 2004.

Bussemer, Thymian, "'Über Propaganda zu Diskutieren, hat wenig Zweck': Zur Medien- und Propagandapolitik von Joseph Goebbels," in Lutz Hachmeister und Michael Kloft (Hrsg.), *Das Goebbels-Experiment: Propaganda und Politik*, München, 2005, 49–63.

Deist, Wilhelm, "The Road to Ideological War: Germany 1918–1945," in Murry Williamson, Macgregor Knox, and Alvin Bernstein (Eds.), *The Making of Strategy: Rulers, States, and War*, Cambridge, New York, 1994, 352–392.

Doob, Leonard, "Goebbels' Principles of Propaganda," in Robert Jackall (Ed.), *Propaganda*, New York, 1995, 190–215.

Eisler, Robert, *Man into Wolf: An Anthropological Interpretation of Sadism, Masochism, and Lycanthropy*, Santa Barbara, 1978.

Fest, Joachim, *The Face of the Third Reich*, New York, 1970.

Fest, Joachim, *Hitler*, London, 1974.

Fest, Joachim, *Inside Hitler's Bunker*, New York, 2004.

Frei, Norbert und Johannes Schmitz, *Journalismus im Dritten Reich*, München, 1989.

Friedländer, Saul, *Nazi Germany and the Jews: Persecution Years, 1933–1939*, New York, 1997.

Fröhlich, Elke, "Hitler und Goebbels im Krisenjahr 1944: Aus den Tagebuchern des Reichspropagandaministers," *Vierteljahrshefte für Zeitgeschichte* 38 (2), 1990, 195–224.

Gellately, Robert, *Backing Hitler: Consent and Coercion in Nazi Germany*, Oxford, NY, 2001.

Gerlach, Christian, "The Wannsee Conference, the Fate of German Jews, and Hitler's Decision in Principle to Exterminate All European Jews," *The Journal of Modern History* 70 (4), 1998, 759–812.

Goldensohn, Leon, *The Nuremberg Interviews: Conversations with the Defendants and Witnesses*, New York, 2005.

Goldhagen, Erich, "Obsession and Realpolitik in the 'Final Solution,'" *Patterns of Prejudice* 12 (1), 1978, 1–16.

Gombrich, Ernst Hans, *Myth and Reality in German War-Time Broadcasts*, London, 1970.

Gutman, Yisrael and Michael Berenbaum (Eds.) *Anatomy of the Auschwitz Death Camp*, Bloomington, Indiana, 1994.

Härtel, Christian, "'Soldat unter Soldaten': Der Journalist Joseph Goebbels," in Lutz Hachmeister und Michael

Kloft (Hrsg.), *Das Goebbels-Experiment: Propaganda und Politik*, München, 2005, 16–28.

Hancock, Eleanor, *The National Socialist Leadership and Total War 1941–1945*, New York, 1991.

Hansen, Reimer, *Das Ende des Dritten Reiches: Die deutsche Kapitulation 1945*, Stuttgart, 1966.

Hecht, Jennifer Michael, "Vacher de Lapouge and the Rise of Nazi Science," *Journal of the History of Ideas*, 2000, 285–304.

Heffner, Sebastian, *The Meaning of Hitler*, New York, 1979.

Heinemann, Winfried, *Operation "Valkyrie": A Military History of the 20 July 1944 Plot*, Berlin/Boston, 2022.

Herf, Jeffrey, "The 'Jewish War': Goebbels and the Antisemitic Campaigns of the Nazi Propaganda Ministry," *Holocaust and Genocide Studies* 19 (1), 2005, 51–80.

Herf, Jeffrey, *The Jewish Enemy: Nazi Propaganda during World War II and the Holocaust*, Cambridge, 2006.

Herzstein, Robert Edwin, *The War that Hitler Won: The Most Infamous Propaganda Campaign in History*, New York, 1978.

Heyen, Franz-Josef (Hrsg.), *Parole der Woche: Eine Wandzeitung im Dritten Reich, 1936–1943*, München, 1983.

Hornshoj-Moller, Stig and David Culbert, "'Der Ewige Jude' (1940): Joseph Goebbels's Unequaled Monument to Antisemitism," *Historical Journal of Film, Radio and Television* 12 (1), 1992, 41–67.

Jäckel, Eberhard, *Hitler's World View*, Cambridge, 1995.

Jersak, Tobias, "A Matter of Foreign Policy: 'Final Solution' and 'Final Victory' in Nazi Germany," *German History* 21 (3), 2003, 369–391.

Joachimsthaler, Anton, *The Last Days of Hitler*, London, 2002.

Kater, Michael, "Inside Nazis: The Goebbels Diaries 1924–1941," *Canadian Journal of History* 25, 1990, 233–243.

Kehrig, Manfred, "Die 6. Armee im Kessel von Stalingrad," in Jürgen Förster (Hrsg.), *Stalingrad: Ereignis-Wirkung-Symbol*, München, 1992, 76–110.

Kershaw, Ian, *The "Hitler Myth." Image and Reality in the Third Reich*, Oxford, 1987.

Kershaw, Ian, *The Nazi Dictatorship: Problems and Perspectives of Interpretation*, New York, 1993.

Kershaw, Ian, *Hitler 1936–1945: Nemesis*, New York, 2000.

Kirwin, Gerald, "Waiting for Retaliation: A Study in Nazi Propaganda Behavior and German Civilian Morale," *Journal of Contemporary History* 16, 1981, 565–583.

Klemperer, Victor, *The Language of the Third Reich: LTI, Lingua Tertii Imperii: A Philologist's Notebook*, London, 2000.

Klemperer, Viktor, *I will Bear Witness, 1942–1945*, New York, 2001.

Kley, Stefan, "Hitler and the Pogrom of November 9–10, 1938," *Yad Vashem Studies* 28, 1999, 73–92.

Krings, Stefan, "Das Propagandaministerium: Joseph Goebbels und seine Spezialisten," in: Lutz Hachmeister und Michael Kloft (Hrsg.), *Das Goebbels-Experiment: Propaganda und Politik*, München, 2005, 29–48.

Kroener, Bernhard, "'Nun, Volk, steh auf ...!' Stalingrad und der 'Totale' Krieg, 1942–1943," in Jürgen Förster (Hrsg.), *Stalingrad: Ereignis-Wirkung-Symbol*, München, 1992, 151–171.

Laqueur, Walter, "Auschwitz," in Michael Neufeld and Michael Berenbaum (Eds.), *The Bombing of Auschwitz: Should the Allies have Attempted it?*, New York, 2000, 186–192.

Lifton, Robert Jay, *Thought Reform and the Psychology of Totalism: A Study of "Brainwashing" in China*, New York, 1961.

Linge, Heinz, *Bis zum Untergang: Als Chef des Persönlichen Dienstes bei Hitler*, München, 1980.

Longerich, Peter, "Joseph Goebbels und der Totale Krieg: Eine Unbekannte Denkschrift des Propagandaministers vom 18. Juli 1944," *Vierteljahrshefte für Zeitgeschichte* 35 (2), 1987, 289–314.

Longerich, Peter, *Goebbels: A Biography*, New York, 2015.

Lukács, Georg, *Die Zerstörung der Vernunft*, Neuwied, 1962.

Massing, Paul, *Rehearsal for Destruction: A Study of Political Anti-Semitism in Imperial Germany*, New York, 1949.

Moltmann, Gunter, "Goebbels's Rede zum Totalen Krieg am 18. Februar 1943," *Vierteljahrshefte für Zeitgeschichte* 12 (1), 1964, 13–43.

Mommsen, Hans, "There was no Führer Order," in Donald Niewyk (Ed.), *The Holocaust: Problems and Perspectives of Interpretation*, Boston, 1997, 27–38.

Mosse, George, *The Crisis of German Ideology: Intellectual Origins of the Third Reich*, New York, 1981.

Mosse, George, *Fallen Soldiers: Reshaping the Memory of the World Wars*, New York, 1990.

Neumann, Boaz, *Nazi World View: Space-Body-Language*, Tel Aviv, 2002.

Noble, Alastair, "The People's Levy—The Volkssturm and Popular Mobilisation in Eastern Germany, 1944–45", *The Journal of Strategic Studies* Vol. 24 (1), 2001, 165–187.

Övermanns, Rüdiger, *Deutsche militärische Verluste im Zweiten Weltkrieg*, München, 2000.

Proctor, Robert, "Nazi Medicine and the Politics of Knowledge," in Sandra Harding (Ed.), *The Racial Economy of Science: Toward a Democratic Future*, Bloomington, 1993, 344–358.

Reich-Ranicki, Marcel, *Mein Leben*, Stuttgart, 2000.

Rose, Paul Laurence, *German Question, Jewish Question, Revolutionary Antisemitism: From Kant to Wagner*, Princeton, 1990.

Rose, Paul Laurence, *Wagner: Race and Revolution*, New Haven, 1992.

Rumpf, Hans, *Das war der Bombenkrieg: Deutsche Städte im Feuersturm*, Oldenburg, 1961.

Sarid, Abraham, "Ricard Wagner and Wilhelm Marr—Harbingers of Modern Antisemitism," *Yalkut Moreshet* 41, 1986, 97–118.

Schellenberg, Walter, *The Schellenberg Memoirs*, London, 1956.

Schmitz-Berning, Cornelia, *Vokabular des National-Sozialismus*, Berlin, 2000.

Speer, Albert, *Erinnerungen*, Berlin, 1970.

Stein, George, *To the Bitter End: The Waffen SS and the Defense of the Third Reich, 1943–45*, New York, 1966.

Steinert, Marlis, *Hitlers Krieg und die Deutschen: Stimmung und Haltung der deutschen Bevölkerung im zweiten Weltkrieg*, Düsseldorf, 1970.

Stern, Fritz, *The Politics of Cultural Despair: A Study in the Rise of the Germanic Ideology*, Garden City, N.Y., 1965.

Trevor-Roper, Hugh, "Introduction," in Hugh Trevor-Roper (Ed.), *Final Entries 1945: The Diaries of Joseph Goebbels*, New York, 1978.

Trevor-Roper, H.R., *Hilter's Last Days*, London, 1978.

Wallach, Jehuda, *The Dogma of the Battle of Annihilation: The Theories of Clausewitz and Schlieffen and their Impact on the German Conduct of Two World Wars*, Westport, Connecticut, 1986.

Wegner, Bernd, "Hitler, der Zweite Weltkrieg und die Choreographie des Untergangs," *Geschichte und Gesellschaft* 26 (3), 2000, 493–518.

Wegner, Bernd (Hrsg.), *Wie Kriege enden: Wege zum Frieden von der Antike bis zur Gegenwart*, Paderborn, 2002.

Weinberg, David, "Approaches to the Study of Film in the Third Reich: A Critical Appraisal," *Journal of Contemporary History* 19 (1), 1984, 105—126.

Weinberg, Gerhard, *A World at Arms: A Global History of World War II*, New York, 1994.

Weindling, Paul, "From Medical War Crimes to Compensation: The Plight of the Victims of Human Experiments," in Wolfgang Eckart (Ed.), *Man, Medicine and the State: The Human Body as an Object of Government*

Sponsored Medical Research in the Twentieth Century, Stuttgart, 2006, 237–249.

Weiss, John, *The Ideology of Death: Why the Holocaust Happened in Germany*, Chicago, 1996.

Welch, David, *The Third Reich: Politics and Propaganda*, London, 1993.

Yahil, Leni, *The Holocaust: The Fate of European Jewry, 1932-–1945*, Oxford, 1990.

Zelinsky, Hartmut, "Decay, annihilation, world rapture," *Zmanim: A History Quarterly* 79, Summer 2002.

Zeman, Z.A.B., *Nazi Propaganda*, London, 1966.

Zimmermann, Clemens, "From Propaganda to Modernization: Media Policy and Media Audiences under National Socialism," *German History* 24 (3), 2006, 431–454.

NAME INDEX

PLACE INDEX

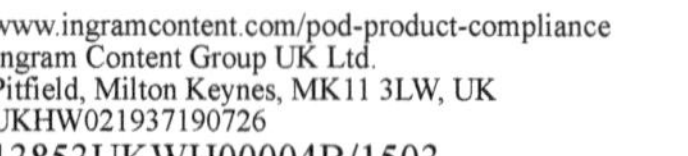

www.ingramcontent.com/pod-product-compliance
Ingram Content Group UK Ltd.
Pitfield, Milton Keynes, MK11 3LW, UK
UKHW021937190726
13853UKWH00004B/1503

9 789655 999013